## PRAISE FOR UNTO LIFE

From the author who helped us redefine the things that really matter in our lives comes an inspired and beautifully written opportunity to see God's hand at work everywhere we turn. *Unto Life* is more than a journey, and more than an observation from a spiritual view. It's uplifting, relatable, and enjoyable to read, with authentic stories from a master storyteller, reminding us to stop and appreciate all that God has done. With the turn of each page, you'll begin to see how every detail in the world around you was designed for your good.

— KAREN MOORE, AUTHOR OF *PRAYERS FROM THE HEART* AND *IT'S STILL POSSIBLE*

John ambles through reflections on daily life in ways that keep drawing us deeper, urging us to pay attention, to see blessings that bloom through the realities and messiness of life. He brings to bear his wisdom as husband and son, pastor and prison chaplain, Bible scholar and dedicated churchman. His wise and steady voice conveys calm and contentment, painting a winsome and stately picture of what it means to live well.

— ARTHUR BOERS, AUTHOR OF *LIVING INTO FOCUS* AND *THE WAY IS MADE BY WALKING*

While I can't endorse everything done today in God's name, I do respect someone who's on a journey for truth like me, someone who invites others to consider spirituality with a gentle tone and accepting heart. *Unto Life* is amazingly beautiful with descriptions that are rich and sumptuous. But most importantly, its spirituality is infused with love.

— MELISSA GILBERT, ACTRESS AND AUTHOR OF
*BACK TO THE PRAIRIE* AND *PRAIRIE TALE: A MEMOIR*

I am so thankful for this book. John invites us to join him in a beautiful conversation about the one thing that's needful. In these pages, you'll discover how *anything*—a dead cell phone, a recreational vehicle, even a romantic comedy—can offer you a way to grow in simple grace. There's also practical advice on things like appreciating your work without being overwhelmed, the need to speak truth to power, and how to rethink spiritual maturity. My favorite part is how the book is a witness to the value of relationships. I consider it a great blessing to fellowship with a conversationalist and wordsmith like John. So, take a deep breath and relax into this exploration of how God wants to bless you along The Way.

— FR. ANTHONY PERKINS, ORTHODOX PRIEST AND
HOST OF THE *ORTHOANALYTIKA* AND *GOOD GUYS
WEAR BLACK* PODCASTS

# UNTO LIFE

## WONDER-FILLED ENCOURAGEMENT FOR THE SPIRITUAL JOURNEY

## JOHN W. MICHALAK

BELLA LUCIA PRESS

The epigraph quotation is taken from George Herbert, *Jacula Prudentum; or, outlandish proverbs, sentences, & c. selected by Mr. George Herbert.* Originally published in 1640.

ISBN: 979-8-9855790-4-8

Edited by Diana Flegal.

Cover design by Kristen Ingebretson. Cover photo by Soft_light.

Author headshot by Leea at AVL Photo.

To learn more about John and his ministry, please visit embracewhatmatters.com.

*For Zolla.*

*The traveling-companion I in no way deserved,*
*but in every way needed.*

*You carry eternity with you wherever you go.*

Life is half spent before we know what it is.

— *GEORGE HERBERT*

# CONTENTS

# HOW TO BEST ENJOY THIS BOOK

To help you best enjoy this book, I wanted to offer a guide on its origin and how it's been organized.

For years, I've been writing spiritual reflections for an online audience. For the most part, this is a collection of those writings.

Normally, a book is written during one season with one theme in mind. But these are mainly random reflections written over two decades. So, the challenge has been to find a vehicle to deliver them to you in a way that's not too confusing and will keep you reading until the end.

Fortunately, in looking back over each reflection, I identified several consistent sub-themes, which you'll see organized under each section. And I discovered one unifying theme—the journey unto life—which I'll explore in the Introduction.

Having said that, it will still help to clarify a few things.

- The writings aren't consistent in length. Some works are brief while others are as long as a feature magazine article.
- The writings vary in style, genre, and tone. Several are devotional. Some resemble a Bible study. There are

many simple life reflections with a spiritual hook. And a number of reflections could qualify as autobiography or personal memoir.

- You won't discover the journey metaphor within many reflections. However, the section introductions should help you see their relevance.

- Finally, you will occasionally read about biographical or world events that appear out of order. This is because the book works best organized by theme rather than chronologically. So, worry less about the order of events than the theme at hand.

As a reader, I always appreciate a roadmap for what's ahead, to know what I'm getting into and what to expect. Despite a few clunky fits, the book has been designed in a way I believe is accessible, encouraging, and resonant to the heart and soul.

So, journey forward with that in mind...

— JOHN MICHALAK

# FOREWORD BY ARTHUR BOERS

For a long time now, I've been hoping to go for a jaunt with John Michalak. He walks on the Smoky Mountain slopes in the Southeastern US and I among the rocks and water terrain we up here like to call the Canadian Shield. As for my aspiration, it could be a long hike or short stroll—no matter. As long as there is ample space for conversation and silence.

We've been growing acquainted for years but have yet to meet face-to-face, something he and I would both prefer. A few years ago, a mutual friend connected us, saying, "I think you two would have a lot to talk about." He was right.

John and I both share a love for Jesus, nature, things pedestrian, scriptures, and helping people live a meaningful, abundant life. Yet we dwell far apart, in different countries even. Thus, we communicate mostly by email. So far nothing face-to-face or side-by-side. We're both still waiting and hoping for that to happen.

While face-to-face and side-by-side are more ideal, I am glad to have a copy of John's latest book, *Unto Life*, in hand. I don't know that this is the "next best thing to being there" (to quote an old commercial that dates me), but it is great nevertheless.

John ambles through reflections on daily life in ways that keep drawing us deeper, urging us to pay attention, to see blessings that bloom through the realities and messiness of life. He brings to bear his wisdom as husband and son, pastor and prison chaplain, Bible scholar and dedicated churchman. I also appreciate his gentle self-deprecating humor. Never trust a spiritual leader who cannot admit and poke fun at his or her foibles.

John loves not just the Word but also words—as we see in his occasional alliteration and always clear writing, not to mention deep and lovely descriptions. Through it all, his wise and steady voice conveys calm and contentment, painting a winsome and stately picture of what it means to live well.

So, if we can't make it to the Smoky Mountains in the near future, at least we can sign on to join him through these lovingly-penned pages.

John makes much of metaphors about journeying. But I would press this even further. He's really talking about pilgrimage—any deliberate and disciplined journey where we go to meet God or God's priorities to be converted by them. He and I have not yet literally walked together, but we're on the same pilgrimage, and I am glad that sooner or later we'll keep each other direct company.

This just has to be.

— Arthur Boers

*Arthur Boers, an Anglican priest in Ontario Canada, is the author of several books, including* Living into Focus: Choosing What Matters in an Age of Distractions.

# INTRODUCTION

Can we sit together a while?

I wish we could meet in person. Maybe we'd sit down one-on-one or with a few friends. At a favorite restaurant or coffee shop. Or maybe it'd be in one of our living rooms or on the back deck, taking in a warm day. We'd laugh and tell jokes. We'd catch up on what's new. We'd listen to each other's stories and bear a few burdens.

We might brainstorm on thoughts of God: a favorite verse, our conclusions or imaginings. We'd air spiritual doubts along with moments of epiphany and recommitment. If we knew each other well, perhaps we'd even lay bare our souls, allowing one another inside those vulnerable places so few others see. We'd encourage each other to keep going and pray for the wisdom and power to get there.

There's nothing like spending time together in person. But if we can't do that, engaging you through a book is a close second. Reading a book is so personal. You can escape the world for moments at a time to encounter an author at the most intimate level—whether he or she is inviting you into their created world or, like me, welcoming you into a conversation about living well.

## TWO DECADES OF REFLECTIONS

Many years ago, I started to write online about living well.

I wrote because I'd wake up with a burden to send a particular something out into the world. I wanted to dive into the depths and surface with something true. True to God. True to me. True to you. Hopefully, all three.

When it happens, you know it. Whether in a book, a sermon, or meaningful discussion, this threefold divine resonance can settle into our hearts, leaving us forever changed. When we wrestle together with God's truth in the laboratory of real-world experience, we can forge a bond that is rich and lasting.

And so, these writings are rooted in God. Formed by years of biblical training and pastoral experience. But this book isn't strictly a Bible study or devotional. These are spiritual reflections rooted within my own story—who I am, where I've been, and... where I'm going.

## UNTO LIFE

> *As by one man's disobedience many were made sinners, so by the obedience of one shall many be made righteous...That as sin reigned unto death, even so might grace reign through righteousness* **unto eternal life** *by Jesus Christ our Lord. (Romans 5:19, 21 KJV)*

Long ago, this little phrase in Romans became a touchstone for me. Where was I headed? Unto life. But not just ordinary life. Unto *eternal* life through Jesus Christ.

This phrase gave me hope—that within my fickle heart with all its insecurity and longing there was a reason to get up in the morning. I finally had someplace to go. A life to pursue. And Jesus was the catalyst who would get me there, sustaining me all the way to the end.

But the phrase also cracked open another revelation. The journey I could take wasn't just focused on the finish line, but also on the quality of life I could experience along the way.

## BOTH THE JOURNEY AND THE DESTINATION

People often have spats over which is more important, the journey or the destination. Many Christians are laser-focused on the end, either heaven or hell, and they often miss out on the holy lessons of the day-to-day. On the flip side, others are so focused on the journey, they end up going nowhere. But both deserve our attention.

Why? Because eternal life doesn't begin when we die and go to heaven. In the mind and heart of God, eternal life has existed before the foundation of the world. But then Jesus came and brought eternity front-and-center for all to see. He began his ministry with the declaration, "The kingdom of heaven is at hand."[1] Heaven wasn't out there somewhere waiting for us. It was thrust into our hearts and minds with the coming of Christ.

So, for followers of Christ, living eternally—in light of the benefits and expectations of God's heavenly kingdom—always begins now. In this way, our journey is intimately linked with our destination. And every step we take can be seen through eternal eyes.

Knowing his kingdom was introduced with the coming of Jesus, we live confident in God, celebrating the victory Christ has achieved. But knowing God's kingdom hasn't yet fully come, we still feel the pain of sin and suffering—in ourselves, others, and in the world. In every step we take, we're empowered by hope for the time God's kingdom will be fulfilled.

That's the spirit of these reflections. How to live eternally: recognizing God's kingdom in this suffering world and serving as an agent in its restoration; overcoming the challenges of stepping out the door and discovering God's power to get you to the finish line.

## WILL YOU JOIN ME?

One of my favorite roles as a servant of God is to *join* and *invite*: to join others in discovering our mutual strengths and weaknesses, our desires and fears; to invite others to join me in better understanding and following the ways of God.

So, grab a comfortable chair. Put your feet up and fold your hands behind your head. The coffee's on and the good snacks are within reach. Let's sit a while, scuttle the small talk, and honor each other with what's real and true.

# PART I
# YOUR PLACE ALONG THE ROAD

On any journey, you need to know where you are.

Sure, it can be exciting to be lost for a time, but if you remain lost, the joy evaporates. Most of the time you need to know both where you are and where you're headed. At any point—you need to know your place.

The phrase, "know your place" often gets a bad rap. We assume we're being put down or locked into some shriveling servitude where we have no value or purpose. But in the journey unto life, knowing your place is both vital and affirming. In addition to showing you where you are, it shows you both where, and to whom, you belong.

One of the first places I go to remember my place is the outdoors—I seek out God's creation.

Far from manmade structures or technology, the filter between me and God is removed. I revel in his beauty. I feel the embrace of his created life. I see his craftwork in the fractal expansion of tree branches and divided streams. I discover his genius in the expanse of color brushed upon skies and landscapes in breathtaking variety. His praises drift along the wind. Birds chirp songs of worship. Bubbling brooks mutter solemn prayers. In nature, this God of eternity doesn't seem far off at all.

*Since the creation of the world* [God's] *invisible attributes, his eternal power and divine nature, have been clearly seen, being understood through what has been made. (Romans 1:20 NASB)*

As we encounter God's created world, we better understand who God is, and who we are, too.

There's no denying God's bigness—the immeasurable scope of his handiwork, everything with a purpose and every part working in harmony. The resonant cycle of life and death. The strategic balance of seasons. Destruction and growth, fruit and scarcity, chaos and peace.

And there's no denying our smallness—how vulnerable we are to the elements, to weather or wildlife or the lack of food or water; the comic difference in scale between us and the Himalayan Mountains or the endless Pacific Ocean.

Within nature, the disparity in power between us and our Creator is made crystal clear. But we aren't belittled in our smallness. We feel welcome, nurtured, truly connected. We better understand our value, our identity, our purpose...our place.

Encountering creation instills in us a confidence that God knows where we are in our journey and has a definitive plan for where we ought to go.

Immerse yourself now within these first reflections about life in the Smoky Mountains. How my time outdoors reminded me of our place in his world, our place along the road, and how fiercely we're connected to him.

# MY HEAD IS BOWED

My head is bowed.

Not because I'm praying, but because I don't want to trip over an unseen rock or upraised root. However, I don't want to miss the larger view either. I want to look up as much as down. Which is a good thing.

I like this hike. The trail has a natural variation in its level paths and uphill grades. It moves from the deep embrace of forest to expansive views of the lake. It has a variety of flowers, plants, and trees. It's long enough to challenge me and short enough to finish in a few hours.

The trail allows me to breathe. Or at least remember I'm breathing. To breathe deeper. Slower. Faster. It feels like I'm the car and someone is filling my tank with the breath of life.

I'm reminded of my body and the way I move. My left foot throbs with a soft pain, alerting me that I must favor one foot over the other. My extra pounds seem heavier, but I don't feel as condemned about my physique as when I'm still. Some people can't walk this trail at all.

*Lord, thank you for my ability to walk.*

Despite my aches and shortness of breath, I remember I'm going somewhere. I'm doing something. My convictions mute my complaints. My laments are diminished by joy.

I feel God. He is not the rock. The tree. The blade of grass or the bird. But he is here. Oh, he is here! His touch is everywhere and infuses me with his peace, his love, his tender care in a way I could never find in a man-made setting. My eyes well up in gratitude.

I worship God by the very act of walking.

My head is bowed.

*You have rescued my soul from death, my eyes from tears, my feet from stumbling. I shall walk before the Lord in the land of the living. (Psalm 116:8-9 NASB)*

# THE LAST HOMELY HOUSE

I t seemed to me at the time that I had stumbled upon the Last
Homely House.[1]

That rainy, misty day, I wandered in my car like Tolkien's Bilbo
on his way to Rivendell. Upward through the North Carolina
mountains, around one bend and still another, I found this small,
50-year-old house perched above 4,000 feet. At this height, the
property was deep within a rain cloud. Surrounded by close-knit
Smoky Mountain summits, it appeared to float upon a lofty,
mystic sea. Like Bilbo, once I'd arrived there, I never wanted to
leave. We purchased the home shortly after.

Today, I write from a back porch where I can see and hear so
many things.

I see tiny mountain homes embedded into the landscape
across airy divides. I see the bulbous, green contour of hills
rolling before me with some other-worldly symmetry. I see the
hills change—under traveling light and shadow, beneath rolling
mists and the horizontal passage of rain clouds. I'm more
immersed in the weather here compared to the distant sea-
level spectator. The sky is more focused as well. The richer colors,

the effect of light, the personality of each visiting cloud. It's no exaggeration to say the heavens here are closer.

Wildlife is abundant. I've spotted a few black bears. White-tailed rabbits roam near the house making me want to pick up the book, *Watership Down,* to discover where they're headed. I've counted at least ten species of birds who are not shy about gorging on our feeders. I see chipmunks and butterflies and black snakes, bumble bees, and benign wasps.

The sounds are constant, but not annoying like in the city. The wind sighs and saunters here and there, roosters crow well beyond waking hours, hound dogs bellow, hummingbirds buzz, other birds chirp and caw and chatter. I hear the sounds of men, but they're distant and often hard to place, whether above or below or from any certain direction. Disembodied voices, lawn-mowers, weed eaters, the slow roll of cars over gravel. It all seems a part rather than an invasive clamor.

I moved to the mountains to pursue Thoreau's deliberate, essential living, to discover what more direct contact with God's creation had to teach me. Whether into the mountains or into God's presence, I'm always longing to go higher and deeper. And now God has granted me a higher place to dwell. To stop and rest, to listen and know. About as high and deep a place as I've ever been able to call home.

Each step brings me closer—from the city to small-town Main Street, from Main Street to this little piece of Rivendell up in the Smokies. Like Abraham, I have some sense of where I should journey next, but am never sure of the more distant destinations.

Now that I'm here, I wonder what new people and purpose await me. Mostly though, I wonder whether this homely, heavenly place will have any lasting effect on my homely, wandering heart.

I'm patient to await such answers. For now, I'll sit on this porch and whisper a prayer of gratitude—that I'd be so privileged to bear witness to this unfiltered glory.

This is my Father's world.
And to my listening ears,
All nature sings, and round me rings
The music of the spheres.

This is my Father's world.
I rest me in the thought
Of rocks and trees, of skies and seas,
His hand the wonders wrought.[2]

# THIS IS MY FATHER'S WORLD

As mentioned, it seemed I had stumbled upon the Last Homely House, and once I'd arrived there, I never wanted to leave.

That is…until I got a look inside.

As much as the world outside looked like Elrond's Rivendell, the inside felt more like Gollum's hellish cave.

Blankets were draped over windows with few lights and low ceilings. The house reeked of cigarettes and dog urine; the walls were murky, the tile and carpet decades old—some rooms floored with just concrete slab. The aluminum window frames were filthy and porous. The bathroom floor was about to fall into the crawl space. It was oppressive just to step inside.

But the opportunity to live amid this astounding mountainous beauty was something we just couldn't pass up. So with the help of subcontractors and friends, we decided to take the leap to restore the house to livable condition. And since moving in, my wife continues to work her magic to make it more livable still.

Despite the darkness of those first impressions, the beauty of creation outside compelled us to make the inside more beautiful, too.

THIS BRINGS to mind the final stanzas of that glorious hymn.

> This is my Father's world.
> Oh, let me ne'er forget
> That though the wrong seems oft so strong,
> God is the ruler yet.[1]

While many recognize the dangers of wasting our lives preoccupied by pleasure or superficiality, we can miss the danger of paying too much attention to the world's darkness. I recognize there's a lot wrong with the world and that wrongs need to be addressed. But my best motivation to address what's wrong is by first immersing my life in what's good and beautiful.

Will I watch the news and despair because all "the wrong seems oft so strong"? No. I will step outside and celebrate the grandeur in these mountains, the encouragements in neighborly kindness, the hope found in houses of worship and charity.

This world is filled with ugliness, but this is my Father's world. And the beauty of his world compels me to join him in addressing the parts in need of restoration.

Despite the work we've already done on this 50-year-old house, it's still far from perfect. Even after remodeling, few of the floors are level. It can be damp and drafty. Doors still need replacing. Walls are desperate for paint. The electricity and plumbing have a mind of their own.

But I can abide by these imperfections. Of course, because of the perfection that lies just outside. But also because I live in hope—that this homely house, my homely heart, and all the world's wrongs can with each passing day bear more resemblance to the beauty of heaven.

And there's even the promise that, one day, I won't even be able to tell the difference.

This is my Father's world.
The battle is not done.
Jesus who died shall be satisfied,
And earth and Heav'n be one.[2]

# THE BLOOM OF WINTER

There's still another reason I moved to the mountains.
Snow.

I love snow. Obsessing over the next snow forecast is one of my chief hobbies during the winter. But snowfall in the southern Appalachians isn't too burdensome. To me anyway. You get a few inches at a time, it melts, and you await the next go around.

Last night, it snowed. The forecasted one to three inches became five, and flurries were still falling after sunrise. I roused my wife, we put on our winter hiking gear, and headed out. Out and up.

One of the benefits of living above 4,000 feet is that after each new snowfall, we have the trails to ourselves. No one without an all-terrain vehicle and some gumption would climb the steep, icy roads to where we already are.

So, this morning it was just the two of us immersed in an untouched winter scene. But then my wife didn't feel well and turned back early. So, soon it was just me, climbing higher, amusing myself with that old Robert Frost poem.

> Whose woods these are I think I know,
> His house is in the village though;
> He will not see me stopping here
> To watch his woods fill up with snow.[1]

But these now felt like my woods. I alone was privileged to trudge up these deep white drifts, to drink in this cold, solitary bliss.

I pulled out my smartphone and started snapping photos of the path, the trees, a mountain stream, and then...

My phone died.

It made no sense. I'd charged it all night so the battery should have been at one-hundred percent. But for all my attempts to power it back up, nothing worked.

A coincidence? Possibly. But my regret prompted the thought that sharing photos may not be the only way to validate my experience with others. And that perhaps my need for validation had too strong a hold on me.

I'VE RECENTLY RETURNED to a study of the spiritual disciplines: activities that help remove what's unnecessary to better enjoy what's real and true—ultimately God himself. There are disciplines of *abstinence*: fasting from food or technology; seeking solitude and silence. There are also disciplines of *engagement*: devotional reading, serving others, worship, and celebration.

This involuntary fast from my smartphone reminded me I didn't need technology to enjoy my surroundings. In fact, without the distraction of documenting my surroundings, I saw things I'd have never appreciated through any man-made lens.

I noticed tracks in the snow that must have come from a deer on the path not far ahead of me. At one point, two hoof tracks became one. The deer must have heard my clumsy approach and fled. So I wasn't as alone as I imagined.

Looking up, I noticed the morning sunlight creating an effect amid the snow-adorned trees—almost like the gates of heaven. But as my eyes pressed downward, a star field of sparkles blazed across the snow beneath my feet—as if the heavens were now upside down.

I noticed the dormant wildflowers. They weren't simply passive, awaiting the spring. Instead, cradles that in warmer months boasted petals of purple, yellow, and red were today filled with white, creating a bloom of winter. Like standing in a field of virgin cotton.

Continuing up, I stopped to catch my breath. And in stopping, I listened. Silence isn't always silent. It can make you aware of the sounds you were missing. Likewise, snow can muffle sound, but it can also accent certain sounds, making them more holy. The baritone song of the wind. The crackle of branches. The flow of melting ice. What if I'd never stopped and listened?

There's a gift in each season. But most, like me, tend to appreciate winter's gift least of all. The world around us is dead. There's more darkness than light. We mourn the chill. Everything seems like it's been put on hold. We're stuck. Waiting.

But here was my reminder that, even when our surroundings are subdued or minimized, life is still life. There's less abundance. We're forced to fast from speeding through our days with abandon. We must stop. Wait. Listen. But God hovers above the void and feeds us with his frozen manna from heaven. He adorns the trees and flowers with his winter bloom, offering us transcendent beauty while the world feels so empty of spectral color.

So often, I stumble upon such revelations about God's world in spite of myself.

I love to hike alone. But this morning, I remembered—the

biggest reason I love solitude is it reminds me that I'm never truly alone. And that these aren't my woods at all.

> Whose woods these are I think I know,
> His house is in *no* village though;
> He *surely* sees me stopping here
> To watch his woods fill up with snow.[2]

# PART II
# WHAT INSPIRES YOU
# TO MOVE

Your journey unto life isn't just from youthful years to old age or from earth to heaven. Your movement is also spiritual, emotional, and mental. Your journey should progress from living life on your own terms to living eternally for God.

So, what inspires you to move toward God? I could speak about many things, but the following reflections explore one source in particular: works of art. Not all works of art. But art that—with the right intention and focus—can inspire in you a longing for something more.

In the mundane drudgery of these meandering days, we need to be inspired. The world feels too tragic, too destined for darkness. We need to believe there is more to life than what's handed to us on the nightly news or reality TV. More in the world, more in others, more in ourselves.

We are three-dimensional beings: body, soul, and spirit. We are also both head and heart. Logic and emotion. God must reach all parts of who we are for us to give our whole selves to him. Artistic works can reach us in ways other stimuli cannot, awakening a devotion to God that helps us live and move and have our being eternally.

Human works of art can have such an eternal effect because we're created in God's image. Humans are born to be mirrors, to reflect God's eternal beauty. When we encounter works like the Sistine Chapel, the stained glass in Notre Dame, the music of Bach, or the books of C.S. Lewis, we find ourselves moved. Moved with joy. Moved with faith and hope. Moved by what we see to live for what is unseen.

Of course, the art doesn't have to be from Michelangelo or Bach. If God can speak through the mouth of a donkey, he can speak through the more common arts, too. The key will be our focus. Whether we're looking to discover divine inspiration in unexpected places as well.

I pray these next reflections will help spark in you a longing for God: through music that bonds you to creation, movies or books that remind you of your role in his story, paintings that help you embrace his beauty, and dramas that offer you a hope that feels genuine and true.

Your journey unto life can find new momentum when you embrace the artistic works of the human race—these creative messengers who inspire us to move toward our Creator.

# FINGAL'S CAVE

Certain works of art have a lifetime impact on you. They shape who you are. For me, reading J.R.R. Tolkien, C.S. Lewis, and Madeline L' Engle as a kid could qualify. Reading the works of Plato in high school was also significant (if that qualifies as art).

One of my most epic encounters with a work of art occurred in my freshman year of college. I was taking a class on *aesthetics*, which refers to the principles of art and beauty. There, I heard a musical composition that will be with me forever.

My earnest professor stood before us one day and said he was going to let us experience the power of musical variation and story. He took a vinyl album from its sleeve, placed it on a record player, and I heard for the first time Felix Mendelssohn's "Hebrides Overture," or as it is also known, "Fingal's Cave."

To better appreciate this music, you must first understand its inspiration. It was 1829 and Mendelssohn was with a friend touring the Scottish island chain known as the Hebrides. The British Isles are often stormy, and this day was no exception. People aboard the paddle steamer were vomiting left and right, including Mendelssohn himself. But the main attraction of the tour was Fingal's Cave. So, despite the storm, he and his friend got into a much smaller boat to enter and explore it.

Fingal's Cave is a 227-foot basalt sea cavern on the Hebrides Island of Staffa. This cave has a color and geological symmetry unmatched in most natural phenomena. Sir Walter Scott described it as:

> One of the most extraordinary places I ever beheld...The sea rolls up to the extremity in most tremendous majesty with a voice like ten thousand giants shouting at once. It exceeded, in my mind, every description I ever heard of it...composed entirely of basaltic pillars as high as the roof of a cathedral, running deep into the rock, eternally swept by a deep and swelling sea, and paved with ruddy marble—[it] baffles all description.[1]

This is the natural marvel Mendelssohn, sick as a dog, encountered in his little boat on that stormy day. And amid these visuals, he also experienced its startling sounds. The acoustics inside the cave with violent waves crashing up and down were, as Scott found, beyond logical description. But as seasick and frightened as he was, Mendelssohn was able to describe it in music.

The record began to play in the classroom. The orchestral strings were at once ominous, recurring, relentless; crashing into the upper reaches of the cave then cascading downward with the high cry of seagulls. The blunt force of melody rose and fell like an incessant wave—rolling, fierce, reaching a terrifying height only to subside into the deepest calm.

As the overture neared its end, there was finally a still in the waters. I thought I was safe. The adventure finished. But then the music ascended again with a tidal assault of storm and sea that left me with no room to breathe. My eyes seeped with tears. I was drowning in blissful wonder. I was in that little boat myself, carried along by the power of nature, left for dead by its terrible beauty.

I NOW LOOK BACK on my experience, and that music's allusion to God and his sovereign power still grip my soul like a vice.

Edmund Burke speaks about such aesthetic encounters. He says:

> The passion caused by the great and sublime in nature…is astonishment: and astonishment is that state of the soul in which all… motions are suspended with some degree of horror. In this case, the mind is so entirely filled with its object that it cannot entertain any other.[2]

In other words, you are so overwhelmed you feel a dread for your existence, but so exhilarated that you're also fully alive. And the object of your focus reigns supreme in your heart and mind.

This is the experience I want to have with God. Through nature and art. Through prayer and worship. He should unsettle me with his surpassing beauty. I should be transfixed by his omnipresent love. In awe of his sublime power.

Since experiencing that one work of art, I've seen God in a profound, new way. I'm on a constant search for similar works that, like Mendelssohn's, might catapult me beyond my finite sense of self into the unbounded presence of my Almighty Creator.

# CHARACTER AND WONDER

I love movies.

For good or ill, they've had a major impact on my life.

I was thinking recently about what makes a great movie... great. There are several ingredients: superb writing, talented actors, a visionary director, striking cinematography. But are there even more intangible qualities that go both deeper and higher, elevating a movie above most others?

Two qualities come to mind—*Character* and *Wonder*. The most impactful movies tend to excel in both of these areas.

The movie *Raiders of The Lost Ark* is one example. The main character, Indiana Jones, is larger than life. He's a brilliant archeologist, handy with a whip, a hard-luck romantic, relentless to a fault. And none of the characters around him are wasted. Even if they just help paint the backdrop of a smelly bar in Nepal or marketplace in Cairo, every character has a vibrant energy and color. And certainly, the world Indy encounters is bursting with wonder: menacing Nazis, exotic locations, and mystic dangers.

In some films, it's the wonder we find in the characters themselves. In *As Good as It Gets*, Jack Nicholson's character is a whirlwind of emotion, a man whose neurotic peccadilloes alienate him from the one thing he wants most—someone to love. And, Helen Hunt, the object of his love, is a wondrous character in the simplest sense. Jack is redeemed by her grounded life, her kindness, her honesty. In this film, the human spirit is a wonder in itself. We're complex, we're simple, we're driven by irrational desire, and we're all crying out for the same things.

In one of my all-time favorite movies, *To Kill a Mockingbird*, we see the innocent character of Scout and the wonder of childhood as she encounters the joys and evils of her small town in Alabama. Her father, Atticus, is a towering wonder of a character —resolute, wise, compassionate. The character, Boo Radley, at first represents all that is fearful in childhood and is defined more by shadow and suggestion. What's revealed though is a grown man with the heart of a child—but also a man with the strength, like Atticus, to protect the weak and stand up for what is right. I could go on and on about the character and wonder found in every frame of this film.

Some readers will remind me that *Mockingbird* is based on Harper Lee's brilliant novel and that these qualities are just as relevant to great literature as they are to movies. I heartily agree. I began this reflection with the medium of film as more people tend to watch movies than read books nowadays. But character and wonder have long been the supreme ingredient in great literature as well.

Which leads, of course, to the greatest storytelling of all, the ancient narratives in the Old and New Testaments. The Bible is a fascinating book in that, while its ultimate purpose is to draw us into an abiding relationship with our Creator, the medium God most often uses is storytelling. And certainly, character and wonder are to be found everywhere in its pages.

Moses, for instance, is quite a character, to say the least. A bag of massive neuroses, he's terribly insecure about his ability to accomplish anything for God and is seen in a comedic scene arguing with the Almighty *ad nauseam* about this fact. He asks,

"Who am I that I should go to Pharaoh and...bring the sons of Israel out of Egypt?"[1]

Like so many of us, Moses knows his character isn't up to the task. But God doesn't deliver a pep talk to build his self-esteem. He asks Moses to focus on something else—the character and wonder of his Creator. God tells him, "I will be with you...I will stretch out my hand and strike the Egyptians with all the wonders I will perform."[2]

God wants Moses to live in a state of wonder as he trusts in the character of his Maker. And in the cinematic fashion we've marveled at in such films as *The Ten Commandments* and *The Prince of Egypt*, God imbues this insecure man with the character to stand up to one of the most powerful men on Earth. Moses delivers over a million people from the bondage of slavery by demonstrating the wonderful miracles of God. He becomes a hero in God's amazing story.

We often go to movies and read books to escape the drudgery of daily living. In those fleeting moments we imagine ourselves the hero, where life is filled with meaning and color, where we're clear about the quest at hand and determined to see it to the end. But then we leave the theater or close the book, and return to what Thoreau called lives of quiet desperation.

But do you realize that God, the author of the greatest story ever told, has included you as a character in his epic quest? An ancient poet said that from your innermost parts you've been "fearfully and wonderfully made."[3] And that for you to play the character God has given you to play, you must simply live in a state of wonder about him and his Son—this "Wonderful Counselor, Mighty God, Eternal Father, Prince of Peace"[4]—this Jesus.

God has written you into his story.

Are you ready to play your part?

# THE USE OF BEAUTY

We have several paintings in our house. Many display poignant scenes of nature. Others are from my parents who spent years painting in watercolors and acrylics. But my favorite painting comes from the Bible. It's a print of Rembrandt's, *The Sacrifice of Isaac.*

In Genesis 22, God asks Abraham to sacrifice his promised son, Isaac, as a test of his faith. The painting shows the climactic moment in this episode. It's a breathtaking example of a still-shot in motion.

Isaac is lying back completely bound. Abraham is gripping Isaac's head to slit his throat with a knife. But in the painting, the knife isn't in Abraham's hand. It's falling. Why? Because Rembrandt captures the exact moment an angel intercedes, grabbing Abraham's wrist to stop the sacrifice and substitute a ram in his stead. Abraham is looking up in stunned surprise. The angel hovers above with a tender urgency. And both Abraham and Isaac are illumined in the glow of the angel's merciful glory.

There are several reasons I love this painting. For one, I've studied the account in Scripture so this event is imbued with meaning by the rest of Abraham's story. But also, the drama of

God's dealings with humanity feels summed up in this one shot. There is faith. Fear. Obedience. Mercy. Provision. Promise.

I love this painting because it is beautiful.

No doubt, it is beautiful because of Rembrandt's talent with paint and color; his ability to tell a tale inside one frame, drawing me in as a nearby observer.

But it's also beautiful because of what it stirs within me. It reminds me of the pain I feel when asked to give up what's most important to me. The uncertainty of following God when the way forward is unclear. The utter shock and relief when God shows unexpected mercy. I marvel that God cared so deeply for Abraham and sense that he cares for me, too.

## WHAT IS PRACTICAL

What is the use of beauty? Most would agree beauty can bring us joy, perhaps entertainment or pleasure. But is there any real use for beauty beyond that?

When it comes to improving our lives, we tend to turn to what is practical. We design gadgets and machines to make things easier and more satisfying. But life usually gets more complicated and less satisfying. And though many advancements in technology and medicine should be celebrated, they're only useful for the life that spans from birth to death. They lead us nowhere beyond. What we see as practical doesn't usually fulfill us in any meaningful way. Not with any effect that is lasting or eternal.

So, what's the use of beauty? Beauty inspires. Beauty elevates. And if something points us to the beauty of God, we can be moved by the breath of his Spirit to live eternally.

> One thing have I asked of the Lord that will I seek after: that I may dwell in the house of the Lord all the days of my life, to gaze upon the beauty of the Lord and to inquire in his temple. (Psalm 27:4 ESV)

There are other paintings I'd love to have on my wall.

One is by Eugène Burnand, showing the apostles Peter and John as they race for the tomb to see if Jesus has truly risen from the dead. In young John's face, we see the look of concerned determination. We know that John later outruns Peter in his frenzy to get there. In Peter's face—who has just days before denied and abandoned Jesus—there is such a mix of emotion it's difficult to describe. Disbelief? Hope? Shame? Passion? All of the above.

Beautiful.

What's the use of such God-focused beauty? While it brings us joy and delight, it can also expose our questions. Our vulnerability. These draw us closer to God in a way clarity and certainty cannot.

God-focused beauty goes beyond the superficial. It affects us deeper than, say, the beauty of a human being or flower garden. As in nature, it awakens us to the deeper truths of who we are. Who we are without God. Who we are with God. It stirs up our need to seek and respond to God. It helps us in our pain. It articulates our prayers.

Despite any doubt and shame, we can find ourselves driven like Peter to run toward Jesus with a resurrected hope. And so beauty not only points us to God, it draws and connects us to God.

## BEAUTY AND CONNECTION

Beauty and connection are interlinked. We already consider beautiful whatever, or whomever, we're connected to.

While they'd be rejected by a New York art critic, tell me you don't proudly hang your child's stickman drawings up on your refrigerator. Old married couples still stare at each other like they're gazing at a supermodel. We'll always find our family beautiful. Our friends, our church, our community, the personal trinkets and décor around the house that tell us we're home.

Beauty offers new connections, too.

> [God] *has made everything beautiful in its time. Also, he has put eternity into man's heart, yet so that he cannot find out what God has done from the beginning to the end. (Ecclesiastes 3:11 ESV)*

> [God] *made from one man every nation of mankind to live on all the face of the earth...that they should seek God, and perhaps feel their way toward him and find him. Yet he is actually not far from each one of us, for 'In him we live and move and have our being.' (Acts 17:26-28 ESV)*

The beauty of God's created world; the beauty of art created by God's image-bearers—these connect us to the mystery of something more. God wants to be found. But we must feel our way toward him. In him, we can live and move and have our being if we'll recognize the beauty that surrounds us and allow it to draw us to him.

## PLEASURES FOREVERMORE

There's another biblical painting we have hanging in our house.

More a sketch drawing, it's called *Jesus and the Lamb* by Katherine Brown, inspired by Isaiah 40:11.

> *Like a shepherd he will tend his flock, in his arm he will gather the lambs and carry them in his bosom; he will gently lead the nursing ewes. (Isaiah 40:11 NASB)*

The image shows Jesus from the shoulders up, holding close a small lamb. The lamb, eyes closed, is nestled deep inside Jesus' neck and face. There is no trace of anxiety or fear, no agenda or care. Only joy, pleasure, and peace.

This one hangs near our door to see whenever we step outside.

God-focused beauty has a knack for digging up the eternal treasures that lie hidden within. Rapturous delight, effusive sorrow, elevated strength. A saturating gratitude for the world that surrounds us and the life we've been given. The desire to search for and cling to what is real and true and lasting. The remembrance of truths we never knew we knew.

> You make known to me the path of life; in your presence there is fullness of joy; at your right hand are pleasures forevermore. (Psalm 16:11 ESV)

What's the use of God-focused beauty? It creates a hunger for something more. A certainty that there *is* something more and that we can experience what that something is.

It helps us live and move and have our being in this beautiful God who's placed our stickman drawings up on his refrigerator, beckoning us to run toward him.

# IN DEFENSE OF FEEL-GOOD STORIES, CHEESY MELODRAMAS, AND HAPPY ENDINGS

I recently completed another viewing of the television series, *Downton Abbey*. Lasting six seasons, it's a melodrama about British high society and servant life set in the early 1900s. I've watched it a few times and am always flummoxed by how the series ends. It's not just a happy ending, but one of the happiest of endings. Every couple is either married off or at least forecast to be married. Most every loose end is tied and every conflict resolved. But what surprises me isn't that the show ends this way, but how truly satisfied I feel because of it.

The enlightened artists of our day have moved away from the black-and-white, Golden age era of happy endings. Usually, for a movie, TV show, or book to be considered a critical success, it must pry open the ribs of our sentimental veneer to reveal the blood-and-guts of true humanity. Life isn't that simple, they say. We're all a horrible mess capable of the vilest evil so we might as well admit it and get on with our lives. And it's certainly no more than a naïve joke to assume that any loose end will be tied or that we'll ever live happily ever after.

Like many cultural protests, there is some truth in these

observations. Humanity has indeed invited a great deal of trouble in trying to maintain masks of perfection, pretending like we have it all together. It is true we're all weak, we all have the potential for evil, and that most events throughout our lives aren't tied up with a tidy bow. So is it just lazy, wishful thinking for me to resonate so deeply with a show that ends well?

Perhaps. I agree there is plenty of simplistic art out there that doesn't reflect true life and the trials of humanity. But one reason I rejoiced at the end of *Downton Abbey* is that, prior to its miraculous ending, the series is full of trials and tribulations I did find believable. Downton wasn't a feel-good series because it's all flowers and daffodils. It felt good because I resonated with both its trials and its resolution.

Maybe it is only the naïve masses who cheer for the feel-good story and happy ending. But within all of us, despite our potential for evil and that complex nuance only appropriate for mature audiences, we still cling to the hope that that isn't all there is. Perhaps within our love of sentimentality there lies a more authentic instinct—that one day, the fairy tale will end as it should.

God's story mirrors this odd cohabitation of hopelessness and hope. Simply glance at Old Testament history and the existential angst of the prophets. You'll find loads of human depravity and open-ended darkness.

But then this Jesus drops into the picture as a bridge between our suffering and hope. He's real about our weaknesses while inviting us to join him in the far-fetched optimism that all will be made well. Jesus took on the full force of our blood-and-guts depravity so we might be present at the story's end: an eternal marriage between God and humanity where everything is tied with a bow that unfathomably rings true.

So, maybe I've just outed myself as one of the lazy, unenlightened gluttons of feel-good entertainment. But my instincts tell me otherwise. Such storytelling may seem sentimental and simple, to be sure. But it can also fill the plot holes in our own stories that hopelessness can't supply.

# PART III
# THE JOURNEY MUST CHANGE YOU

On any significant journey, change is inevitable.

Not the more minor trips, like a weekend away or a weeklong itinerary. But on the longer expeditions where you travel through sites challenging and unknown, you'll likely find yourself changed.

In my college days, I studied in England and backpacked around Europe for a time. When I returned to the United States, I wasn't the same person. My perspective was stretched by experiencing so many diverse cultures and meeting people who didn't live or see the world the way I did. I even viewed my own country in a different light, having observed it from afar for a while.

Your journey unto life will be long and significant. It will change you. But to be blunt—the journey must change you or you're probably not walking the road God intends. Along the path unto life eternal, change is woven into the fabric of both the journey and the destination.

*Unless one is born again, he cannot see the kingdom of God. (John 3:3 NASB)*

*If anyone is in Christ, he is a new creation. The old has passed away; behold, the new has come. (2 Corinthians 5:17 ESV)*

To even begin the journey, you must be born again and become a new creation. Along the way, your new spiritual identity will come to the surface through the long cycle of discipleship, transformation, disobedience, repentance, and renewal.

And once you finally reach your destination, change awaits you there, too.

*The dead will be raised imperishable, and we will be changed. (1 Corinthians 15:52 NASB)*

The following writings reflect on this change—this transformation from death unto life.

You must begin in spiritual infancy where you humble yourself as a little child. You must then turn a magnifying glass on your heart and uncover any obstacles resisting your change. You must seek the encouragement for love and good deeds that come from Christian community. And when you're about to give up, you must remember that God is in the business of breathing life into your dusty frame to transform you into something new for his glory.

How you start isn't how you'll finish. The journey must change you—from beginning to end.

# GROWING UP AGAIN

*There exists in most men a poet who died young while the man survived. —*
*Sainte-Beuve*[1]

It is one of the gifts of life to me that no matter how old we are, we're never far from the glory and imagery of childhood.

We spend about a quarter of our life as children. Then many have children of their own and raise them into their middle years. Their children then have children, and if they're granted years beyond the average span, their greatness is measured by how many generations of children surround them.

For people like me and my wife, we have the gift of nieces and nephews, the children of friends and extended family. So, unless we're monks or hermits, children are always around us.

Most of the benefits from this gift are obvious. Some are beyond comprehension.

Children infuse our decaying psyches with the pulse of renewal, innocence, and purity. They shock us out of the mundane drone of anxious reality into living in the rapturous present. They remind us of guileless friendship and interdimensional joy. Their life's purpose is seated in love and connection.

Imagination isn't a word they use. It's the lens through which they see everything.

And too, children remind us of the dual nature in all human beings: the selfish passion to have our own way; the angelic glory found in wonder, hope, and humility.

Scripture speaks of the lessons of childhood—what it means to be a child and what it means to grow up. But we often exempt ourselves from these lessons, because as adults we don't think we need them anymore. But no matter our age, we're never beyond needing them.

Most reading this have reached adulthood. You have a job, you pay your taxes, you take out the trash. You've left your father and mother and have some sense of control and independence in the life you live.

But what about your spiritual life? Are you likewise a spiritual grown-up, not needing a heavenly Father to protect you and help make sense of things? Spiritually, no matter your sense of maturity, shouldn't you always remain like a child, looking with unknowing awe and dependence toward your daddy?

Scripture does say you must grow spiritually. But most of us stunt this growth because we won't first regress into spiritual infancy. We think the goal should be to learn self-confidence. Control. Independence. But Christ said we must first humble ourselves and seek him with all the dependence and frailty of a little child.

Perhaps you've grown spiritually in some areas but are still a child in others. Or perhaps you learned an important lesson early on, but now that you're mature, you've forgotten what it was. God often calls us backward to move us forward.

As an adult, you should, of course, manage many areas of life with responsibility and restraint. But spiritually, don't neglect the uninhibited passion of childhood—to embrace all God has to offer; to cry out to God when things aren't so good.

Growing up can be hard and there are memories of youth you

wouldn't want to repeat. But we serve a God who makes all things new. The kingdom of heaven is found not in the security of adulthood, but in the precarious wonder of starting over with a remembered innocence.

So whatever your age, your future depends on not just being born again, but also growing up again.

And as we grow up again in him, we are called children of hope and promise.

*See how great a love the Father has bestowed on us, that we would be called children of God. And such we are...It has not appeared as yet what we will be. [But] we know that when he appears, we will be like him, because we will see him just as he is...everyone who has this hope fixed on him purifies himself, just as he is pure. (1 John 3:1-3 NASB)*

# EIGHT QUESTIONS

*If you continue in my word, then you are truly disciples of mine; and you will know the truth, and the truth will make you free. (John 8:31-32 NASB)*

To read the Bible is to learn the truth about God. But it's also to learn the truth about yourself.

The truth is there is a God who loves and cares for you, who has spent human history intimately engaged in the restoration of mankind to himself, ultimately through the birth and sacrifice of his Son. The truth of this loving, just, and merciful God is revealed throughout Scripture.

But Scripture also reveals the truth about you and me. We're not God. But we try to be. We too often live life on our own terms. The Bible exposes our true selves over and over, "piercing as far as the division of soul and spirit...able to judge the thoughts and intentions of the heart."[1]

Certainly, our utmost focus and devotion should be upon God. But such devotion is best energized through relationship—and a relationship has two sides. It's possible for our devotion to be inauthentic if we don't get real about our side of things in knowing ourselves deep down.

*Examine yourselves to see whether you are in the faith. (2 Corinthians 13:5 ESV)*

IN MY YEARS working with men in prison—many who never took an honest look at themselves—I came up with eight questions that would start them on the road to discovering the truth about God and them.

And so, I will ask you these questions as well.

While the questions must begin with you, you must ask God to help reveal the answers. If you've never done such self-examination, know that most answers won't come right away, but over time as you ask God to reveal them.

## QUESTION 1: WHO ARE YOU?

This is a question about your self-awareness and identity. How do you define yourself? If you've let others define you, how has that felt? A sense of personal identity affects the way you think, speak, and live. Jesus knew who he was. His identity was the bedrock of everything he said and did.

*I am the light of the world. He who follows me will not walk in darkness, but have the light of life. (John 8:12 NASB)*

## QUESTION 2: WHY ARE YOU HERE?

This question is about your direction and purpose. Why are you here on this planet? Why were you born at this time and place?

What are you meant to accomplish in the time you have left? Without a sense of purpose, your life will always be adrift.

*Purpose in a man's heart is like deep water, but a man of understanding will draw it out. (Proverbs 20:5 ESV)*

## QUESTION 3: WHAT DO YOU WANT?

This question points to your will or desires. What do you want out of life? If you're unsure, the best evidence for what you want is what you think, say, and do. Some of your desires will be healthy and good. Some will be unhealthy and not so good. Be honest about the desires that lie within you.

*When Jesus saw him lying there and knew he already had been in that condition a long time, he said to him, "Do you want to be made well?" (John 5:6 NKJV)*

## QUESTION 4: IS THERE A DIFFERENCE BETWEEN WHAT YOU SAY YOU WANT AND HOW YOU'RE LIVING YOUR LIFE?

This question examines your character and integrity. When what you want is good, do your desires match your actions?

*I have the desire to do what is good, but I cannot carry it out. For I do not do the good I want to do, but the evil I do not want to do—this I keep on doing. (Romans 7:18-19 NIV)*

## QUESTION 5: WHAT DOES GOD WANT?

This question addresses your consideration for God and others. If your focus has been on yourself, why is this? Who is the center of your universe? This is more than just a question of knowledge. It's a question of submission.

> 'Love the Lord your God with all your heart, and with all your soul, and with all your mind.' This is the great and foremost commandment. The second is like it, 'You shall love your neighbor as yourself.' (Matthew 22:37-39 NASB)

## QUESTION 6: IF YOU WANT WHAT GOD WANTS, WHAT ARE YOU WILLING TO DO TO GET IT?

This question measures your discipline and commitment. For many of us, following Christ is more about wishful thinking than determined action. Choosing an easy life in the moment often leads to a difficult life in the long run. The call to discipleship is often more difficult from day to day, but it leads to a long-term life of peace, purpose, and stability.

> Whoever wishes to save his life will lose it; but whoever loses his life for my sake will find it. (Matthew 16:25 NASB)

## QUESTION 7: WHO ARE YOU BECOMING?

This question evaluates your belief and vision. Most of the time we can't believe in God and walk in his steps until he first believes in us. You need godly people around you who—while accepting you as you are—have a vision for who you can become.

> Jesus said to [the woman caught in adultery], "I do not condemn you... From now on sin no more." (John 8:11 NASB)

## QUESTION 8: WHO ARE YOU WITH?

This is a question about your relationships. Who you are with will affect your answer to every preceding question. If you're not growing in relationship with God and those asking similar questions, you won't discover your true identity and purpose. You won't learn God's will or live a life of integrity and discipline. And you won't become who God wants you to be.

> *Moses said to God, "Who am I that I should go to Pharaoh and bring the Israelites out of Egypt?"* [God] *said, "I will be with you." (Exodus 3:11-12 NIV)*

As we look to God and Scripture, we will find all the answers we need.

But every answer begins with a question.

# CLASS IS ALWAYS IN SESSION

When I was in school, I never thought I'd miss it. But, I do now. Life had more structure: a strict schedule, expectations and goals, and a clear measure of success or failure.

Outside school, it's all been up to me. I must structure my life (or not). Any expectations or goals are generally of my own making. And whether my life is a success or failure is often far more difficult to pin down.

But there's another reason I miss school. It reminds me that, while in the environment of teaching and learning, I have a much stronger motivation to live well.

Since leaving school I've been a teacher, preached sermons, and led many Christian classes and seminars. When I'm teaching moral principles—from how to better follow Christ or have a better marriage—I'm more motivated to live out those principles myself.

The same can be said for parenting. When that baby first appears in the delivery room, most parents feel a deep-seated conviction to live more responsible lives. After all, how can they raise a child to be moral and mature if they too aren't living that way? This isn't to say parents always succeed in this. But the motivation is there just the same.

While not a parent, this fear of hypocrisy dogs me. When I'm not teaching others or learning from others, it's too easy to fall off the wagon and not pursue the life-change God intends. So what right do I have to tell others how to live?

This isn't an empty question. We can't ask others to walk a certain path when we ignore the wisdom we're imparting. However, the other extreme produces a paralyzing self-condemnation: we're so defeated for not living well when it's just up to us, we may be tempted to never live well again.

But here's the thing. Even if you're no longer in school—class is always in session. By your example and lifestyle, you're always teaching others something. And by what you allow inside your heart and mind, you might as well still be a student sitting behind a desk.

So if class is always in session, the question you must ask is: *What kind of school do I want to attend?*


## THE SCHOOL OF GOD

Not surprisingly, the writer of Hebrews invites us to enroll in the school of God.

> *Let us consider how to stimulate one another to love and good deeds, not forsaking our own assembling together as is the habit of some, but encouraging one another; and all the more as you see the day drawing near. (Hebrews 10:24-25 NASB)*

The school of God is not just independent study.

It's telling that the first problem God had to address in human history wasn't sin. It was *isolation*. Before the fall ever occurred, God said, "It is not good for man to be alone."[1] While there are some individual qualities to life's journey, we are not meant to grow and mature in isolation. And more often than not, it's our aloneness that stirs up our fallenness.

When I'm teaching and learning from others, I'm much more motivated to improve and live well. The fact that I don't live as well outside such environments is no reason for self-condemnation. The classroom of community—or better said, the school of divine love—is simply the greatest motivator to live my best life for God and others.

So, whether it's through a church, Bible class, support group, workout group, or community service project; whether it's parenting, mentoring, or through meaningful friendships—God is calling you back to school. Let your learning and teaching be founded in a godly, biblical worldview. But always be learning. Always be teaching.

What was that? Did you just hear the bell ring?

Class is in session again.

# RECREATIONAL VEHICLES

Many people want to pay off their mortgage and retire so they can do one thing: purchase a recreational vehicle and hit the road. My parents did this several years back: traveling the country, working at different camps, enjoying the good life. My wife and I have often whispered of selling all we own, buying an RV, and heading out into the unknown.

RV life is an adventure. You trade your ordinary, predictable world for a life of scenic beauty and imagination. The sunrise is always before you. There is a richness and vitality in the people you meet, the places you see, in the potential to start each day anew. The very word *recreational* speaks of a life of refreshment and joy. You just need a vehicle to get you there.

IT OCCURS to me that you and I are recreational vehicles. Or at least we can be if we'll change our focus and see ourselves with different eyes.

Did you realize God's activity throughout most human history hasn't been so much creative as "re-creational"? Only the first few pages in the Bible narrate God's activity as Creator (despite retrospective allusions elsewhere).

The rest of the story—from the time God forms man from the dust of the ground and breathes into his nostrils the breath of life —involves recreation. The transforming of ordinary or fallen material into something sanctified and glorious.

My own story is a microcosm of this recreation. Through God's breath into my dusty frame, strength and reconciliation have arisen from a life of weakness and brokenness. Passion and purity have been birthed from a past of apathy and illicit desire. God continues my transformation still, and will continue it for his glory.

People bemoan that they've never experienced the miracles of old—the parting of the Red Sea, sight to the blind, the dead rising from the grave. But they're ignoring the miracles that occur every day, right under their nose.

Have you ever witnessed someone's character transform from a life of selfishness into a life of service to others? Or perhaps a sexually-abused girl who now brings spiritual healing to those in similar pain? Have you ever seen a lifeless marriage that rediscovers love, forgiveness, and intimacy? If you claim these kinds of events aren't miracles, you aren't paying attention.

Most miracles only appear supernatural to us. But they're simply the Creator transforming—or recreating—something without promise into something new and glorious. From the lifeless seed of Abraham's body, Sarah birthed a child, decades beyond what was considered natural. How? Because Abraham trusted in the God who "gives life to the dead and calls the things that are not, the things that are."[1] The impossible became possible. What was unseen was seen.

Do you spend your days in meaningless drudgery, longing for the time you'll get to buy an RV and enjoy the good life? Or worse, do you see only how ordinary and fallen you are, only a world of darkness, suffering, and brokenness? It's naive to deny such darkness exists. But if you simply shift your focus, you don't have to wait for the good life to begin. There is a light that can transform everything you are and everything you see.

There's nothing wrong with owning a recreational vehicle. But the better dream is to *be* a recreational vehicle. To leave the past in the rearview mirror and travel the adventurous road. To journey toward this faithful Creator who offers you a new heart and a new spirit, who calls the things we believe are not—the things that are.

You have only to turn around to leave the darkness behind.

The sunrise awaits.

# PART IV
## STAYING CONTENT ALONG THE WAY

I'll admit when it comes to long road trips, I care far more about the destination.

We've decided to go somewhere—to see family, a nice vacation, perhaps a conference or retreat. And that's my focus. I won't relax and enjoy our travels until I get there.

My wife also values the destination, but she wants to enjoy the journey as well. If she had her way, we'd take all the back roads from North Carolina to New Mexico. We'd stop at every small town. Every fruit stand. Every antique shop. We'd pause to enjoy the local cuisine. We'd sit in rocking chairs and chat with the locals without a care in the world.

Now, while we'll most often differ on road trips, I must concede that my wife has a better sense of how to travel eternally. As mentioned, to walk in step with the benefits and expectations of God's kingdom, the journey must carry the same weight as the destination.

Spiritually, you should certainly place a high value on where you're headed—a future of heavenly contentment, joy, and peace.

But too many of us won't be content until we get there. We're unhappy with our job or with family and friends. We're disgruntled with our weight or physique or with how much money we have in the bank. We're bitter about our past; we're unsatisfied with our present. We blame others or God for our circumstances. We look at everyone else's perfect lives and wonder why we can't be happy too.

When you live in such discontentment, you'll miss so much of what God wants to give you in your journey. And you'll be the poorest example to those who crave the contentment only eternal hope can bring.

*Why are you in despair, O my soul? And why have you become disturbed within me? Hope in God, for I shall again praise him for the help of his presence. (Psalm 42:5 NASB)*

Staying content while you journey is not about making God into a slot machine where success is defined by riches and pleasure. And it's not about putting on a happy face when things are in the pits. The contented life is about recognizing that God started you out along this path and—despite your highs and lows, despite your present understanding—he knows best how to live in joy and peace.

In these next reflections, I explore ways to pursue what nurtures eternal contentment and how to leave behind what doesn't.

The destination is absolutely worth reaching. But don't forget to enjoy the rocking chairs and fruit stands along the way.

# MINDING YOUR P'S

No need to tell you where I was—but it was wonderful.

It was high summer and I was on vacation, visiting a location I'd seen many times before. The sun was setting. I was standing alone on a quiet country road at the head of an expansive bean field. The crop was low and plush, allowing me to see all the way to the end. The fading sunlight had been replaced by dozens of fireflies, pulsing their glow over the field with a soft, glorious caress. I could barely catch my breath for the reverence of the moment. It was a pocket of earth pregnant with peace and innocence, a place where you could smell the organic fruit of pure and unadulterated life. For me, there was no other place like it on earth.

Now, there are many sunsets, bean fields, and fireflies out there, so why was this location so special? Because, for me, it was more than just a place. Long ago, it was there where I'd found a *sense* of place. It was there where I'd found a community of people who changed who I am. It was there where I'd discovered my first glimpse of purpose. On that high summer evening, I was awed not just by a scenic location. A sense of Place. People. Purpose. That's what made it special.

This experience reminded me that, while we're told to mind our *P's & Q's* (an old idiom that calls us to use our best manners), perhaps our decorum would be better informed by spending time just on our P's: Our sense of place, people, and purpose. Our Q's, whatever those may be, might be examined later.

Often we get to enjoy just one or two of these P's at a time, so we float adrift through life, wondering what's missing. Have you ever had a satisfying sense of people or community—a great marriage, kids, church, friends—but hated the place where you lived? Have you ever had a satisfying sense of community, maybe even loved where you lived, but had no strong sense of purpose? We can go through all the combinations, but you get the picture. We're most content when we experience all three.

However, one question is: If you don't enjoy all three, what do you do? Just live in discontentment and anguish?

There are different ways to approach this.

A sense of place, people, and purpose can be discovered. Some may miss them simply because they haven't searched hard enough. You might stumble upon them in your journey as I did.

It's possible to realize they've been there all along. We just need to broaden our perspective to see it.

For instance, at the time of this writing, while generally happy, I'm a bit disgruntled that I may never carry out my purpose or live in a place that fits me. But then I remember: I love my wife and she loves me. Our marriage is the most important sense of community I could ever have. Wherever we are, she always gives me a strong sense of place. In many ways, loving her well is my best sense of purpose. I'm sure those of you with kids, grandchildren, or good friends could say the same. So often we pursue the three P's outside those who love us, and we're the emptier for it.

In light of that, our most important area of focus should be on God. I love God and he loves me. No matter where I hang my hat —he is with me. He provides my truest sense of place. My dependence on him and his people gives me a sense of community no matter where I'm at or what I'm doing. Serving God and those in need should always be my most enduring purpose. We can lose track of this and try to mind our P's apart from God. But then life makes no sense.

Certainly, we should recognize his divine nature in the places, people, and purposes of this world. That's what made the three P's I experienced above so special. Long ago, amidst that place of twilight, bean fields, and fireflies, I first heard God invite me to join his people and discover my spiritual purpose. It was there where his touch on creation left an overwhelming reminder of his place in my life. There, like no other place on earth, I knew I was home and had a glimpse of my eternal home.

Where are you? Who are you with? Why are you here? I hope you're seeking to answer these questions with some measure of satisfaction. If not, start your search for all three. Pursue them. Pray for them. Step back and see how they've been there all along. Ground your most organic sense of place, people, and purpose in God and in Jesus, his Son.

Are you minding your P's? It's not just about good manners.

Life doesn't make much sense without them.

# AWAKENING FROM THE AMERICAN DREAM

*(WRITTEN DURING THE 2008 ECONOMIC CRISIS)*

I hate to admit this, but I'm sometimes captivated by the idea of oncoming upheaval.

It's not that I welcome the suffering a crisis can bring. But it often serves as a wake-up call for humanity to get its priorities back in order.

That's one of my thoughts as I observe the current disruption in our country's economy. I see people writhing in pain and gnashing their teeth at the gas pump and on the floor of the U.S. Stock Exchange. For some, the anxiety is justified. For others, it isn't.

The nightmare too many of us fear is sourced in a corrupt mutation of what was once a good dream—the American Dream.

For those in the United States, the American Dream grew out of the right to life, liberty, and the pursuit of happiness. Our founders believed that everyone should be afforded the opportunity to make a life for themselves, to pursue contentment and, dare I say, meaning and purpose.

But what truly brings us happiness? Is it the freedom to use our credit card for daily expenses and make only the minimum payment every month? Is it to endlessly pursue the latest fashion, smartphone, or high-definition TV? Is it the opportunity to build equity in a home only to buy an even larger home? Is it acquiring so many material goods that both parents must work full-time and rarely see each other or their kids?

I don't claim to be above the attractions of materialism. But I do consider myself an addict working the steps toward recovery. Over the last few years, I've moved from holding a nice corporate job I felt was devoid of meaning to seeking a life in service to others. My wife and I currently work part-time, continue to minimize what we own, and are looking to prioritize our lives as best we can.

Our first year in this experiment was one of the happiest in our marriage. We saw an immediate payoff in distancing ourselves from a material-obsessed culture. For instance, we often had little money for the mortgage just a few days before it was due. But every month without fail, the money came in. We were happy in one sense because money wasn't something to argue about. We didn't have any!

I understand not everyone will have this experience, but it helped us evaluate what we really need to be happy. If we live in constant fear of losing everything, is it possible our definition of *everything* may be a tad misguided? You've heard that people who lose their house in a fire remember what's most important. The loss of money or material possessions can wake us up to what matters.

The American Dream, in its purest ideal, is a worthy goal. But without a more solid foundation, it can lead to the nightmare we're experiencing today.

There's a deeper dream, a richer happiness worth pursuing. A *Kingdom Dream*, if you will. As an observer of Jesus and what he did when he walked our soil long ago, I see a King with a

Kingdom Dream. But it wasn't a dream of riches, comfort, or retirement.

Jesus was, in the most practical sense, a homeless man. He had no large home, nor did he have a large mortgage. He traveled from place to place in service to others. He had little to no money. What he did have, he shared with his community and those he traveled with.

He had no internet, no television, no smartphone to distract him from the real world. He had no car. He walked everywhere. His pace was slower. He noticed and embraced the world around him. Sure, he paid his taxes to Caesar, but he wasn't obsessed with how his taxes were spent. He made his most important investment in the kingdom of God.

During this economic crisis, folks are asking whether a bunch of greedy, materialistic corporations should be bailed-out by our government with the hope that our economy won't go under. I go back and forth on this issue and will let better minds debate it among themselves.

But what gives me the most peace is that this King living his Kingdom Dream offered me—a greedy, materialistic human—a bail-out that goes much further than any temporary band-aid for our economy. Christ lost everything so I could have him, who truly is everything.

And Christ's rescue wasn't only about a future contentment in heaven. He offered me life, liberty, and the pursuit of happiness in a kingdom that is present today, at hand in the here-and-now. He offered a kingdom that exists in the eyes of the poor in spirit, in the humble of heart, in the peacemaker, in the ones who love God and others more than themselves.

That's a happiness worth pursuing. As long as we're willing to awaken from the nightmare.

As scary as any nightmare can be—upon waking, it soon seems brief, fleeting, and is soon forgotten.

# WHAT'S YOUR WORKING RELATIONSHIP?

Do you like what you do? According to recent surveys, most Americans don't. Many are unhappy and wish they were somewhere else. Some are lazy. Others unchallenged. Some can't get along with their boss or co-workers. Others feel unappreciated for all they do.

If we're not happy with what we do, it might be time for some self-examination. Why? Because how we relate to work defines who we are as human beings. The concept of work is sewn into the fabric of life's purpose and meaning.

## WHAT THE BIBLE SAYS ABOUT WORK

In the Bible, the first thing we read about God doing is work. When he speaks, he does so with a view toward productivity. He produces light, earth, sea, plants, animals, and humans—all with a reproductive and practical purpose. The first commission he gives mankind is to cultivate and maintain Eden. And so, our purpose from the very beginning has typically been exercised through work.

The Bible also has a lot to say about how we should relate to our work.

Do you feel unappreciated at your job (outside or inside the home), that no one affirms or rewards what you do? There are many biblical passages where God defends fair pay and justice in the workplace. But he also wants our earthly attitude to reflect an eternal mindset. God says it's better to be a nobody who employs others than to starve with nothing to feed you but your ego.[1] Ultimately, he's the one you should be working for. He's the one you should seek your rewards and recognition from.[2]

The Bible says that work produces, and idleness, believe it or not, destroys.[3] When we have nothing to do for an extended period, our love turns inward and our judgment, outward.[4] When we aren't producing, we're more apt to live in fear and even lose what God meant for us to put to good use in the first place.[5]

You've heard the stories of people who win the lottery only to collapse into bankruptcy, broken relationships, and even death? God says that "the wealth of a diligent man is precious."[6] Work produces an appreciation for what we have. With unearned wealth, our possessions can become worthless. We continually crave good things, but are left with nothing.[7]

Now, it's true that God gives us our most precious possession —eternal life—through his grace and not through our own works. But, while freely given, this grace is offered because of the finished work of God's Son. And so in response to this grace, we'll have no true contentment without following the same work-ethic Jesus had while here on earth.

When we accept the rewards of Christ's work, we do so by signing a new job application. God becomes our new boss. He's already paid us the highest of salaries and promises to help us accomplish work we could never do on our own.[8] But as seen in the first pages of Genesis, God expects our focus to be on repro-ducing in others what he has produced in us.

If you're feeling disgruntled with your job, with the effort you produce, with your place in life, ask yourself this question: What are you working for? Is it to earn a paycheck, to put food on the table, to buy shoes for the kids? This is right to do. But realize that you were created to work for more than just you and your family.

God says our efforts should also benefit those in need, whether physical or spiritual.[9] He says a person should "labor, performing with his own hands what is good, so he will have something to share with one who has need."[10]

Our relationship to work, then, should have everything to do with how we work on our relationships.

What if you applied the following counsel as a work ethic, both on the job and in life itself?

*Love from the center of who you are; don't fake it. Run for dear life from evil; hold on for dear life to good. Be good friends who love deeply; practice playing second fiddle. Don't burn out; keep yourselves fueled and aflame. Be alert servants of the Master, cheerfully expectant. Don't quit in hard times; pray all the harder. Help needy Christians; be inventive in hospitality. Bless your enemies; no cursing under your breath. Laugh with your happy friends when they're happy; share tears when they're down. Get along with each other; don't be stuck up. Make friends with nobodies; don't be the great somebody. Don't hit back; discover beauty in everyone. If you've got it in you, get along with everybody. (Romans 12:9-18 MSG)*

Tell me the effort described above wouldn't produce a reward that is miles beyond a fair paycheck and job recognition. It would both exhaust you and help you sleep more soundly at night. It would produce in you and others a life of purpose, contentment, and meaning.

Whether you've noticed it or not, God has placed a sign in the window of your soul:

"Help Wanted."

What are you ready to do for him?

# THE RESTORATION OF LOST DREAMS

What if you reached the end of your days and never received what you most desired?

Would you conclude life had no meaning and spend your remaining time in selfishness and pleasure? Would you give up on God or even decide he was never there in the first place?

I've felt this temptation at times. Now in my 50s, for instance, I've given up on the dream that my wife and I will have our own children. We're still considering foster care and perhaps adoption, but the pain of that lost dream still haunts me. I've wanted my own children for as long as I can remember. This and other dreams haven't come to pass in the way I expected.

So what if God doesn't fulfill our deepest longings and dreams?

## LONGING IN SCRIPTURE

One bit of hope we discover is that God isn't deaf to such questions. The scriptures tell many stories of loss and longing, the pain of waiting, and how God wants us to understand both the problem and the solution.

The first loss we see is in Eden. When Adam and Eve sin and are cast out of the paradise they know and love, their dream of eternal life and unfiltered companionship with God are no more.

Like my wife and me, Abraham and Sarah suffer the lost dream of children throughout much of their lives. Job loses nearly everything he holds dear. Joseph loses his freedom with no hope in sight. King David suffers the loss of sons and family. Solomon feels the loss of meaning and purpose. Jeremiah mourns the loss of Israel's faithfulness and its homeland in Jerusalem. Over and over again, God's people long for what could have been and wonder if happiness will always remain out of reach.

Of course, some dreams in Scripture are eventually restored, but many aren't. Some are restored, but not completely or according to expectation. But even for those who experience restoration, most wait years to see it, never knowing whether it will come to pass at all.

And so for most, the true test of faithfulness is in the waiting.

## CONTENTMENT THROUGH THE LONG LENS

The loss experienced in Eden finally discovers new hope with the coming of Christ. Looking upon the baby Jesus, Simeon, who has spent his whole life waiting for the consolation of Israel, says, "Lord, you are releasing your bond-servant to depart in peace... for my eyes have seen your salvation."[1]

Jesus later proclaims that the kingdom of heaven is indeed at hand. But knowing the dream hasn't yet been fully realized, he directs his disciples to let their contentment be defined through the long lens.

> Blessed are the poor in spirit, for theirs is the kingdom of heaven. Blessed are those who mourn, for they shall be comforted. Blessed are the gentle, for they shall inherit the earth. Blessed are those who hunger and thirst for righteousness, for they shall be satisfied. (Matthew 5:3-6 NASB)

In the Beatitudes, God both identifies with our hopelessness and offers us hope. Like in the Old Testament, many hearing Jesus' words will see some restoration in their lifetime. Others won't see it until after they die. That's the tension we all must negotiate with our own lost dreams. The kingdom of heaven is here already. But it hasn't been fulfilled quite yet.

And so, the word I believe Jesus emphasizes in Matthew is, *blessed*. As we await the future fulfillment of God's promises, God says it's still possible to be blessed. To know contentment in the here-and-now.

Why? Because faithfulness has its own reward. Because the Holy Spirit offers us a deposit on our future inheritance, a taste of future bliss that satisfies our heart and mind. While we may have to wait for the restoration of all things, we don't have to wait to know God loves us beyond imagining and sacrificed his Son so that the lost dream of Eden would be restored. In this sense, our contentment can have an eternal quality that rises above any highs and lows.

Paul said:

> *I have learned to be content in whatever circumstances I am. I know how to get along with humble means, and I also know how to live in prosperity; in any and every circumstance I have learned the secret of being filled and going hungry, both of having abundance and suffering need. I can do all things through him who strengthens me. (Philippians 4:11-13 NASB)*

In my view, verse 13 here contains a mistranslated word. The Greek word for *can* in "I *can* do all things" also means, *strong*. Within the context of Paul's letter, I believe it's more accurately translated, "I am *strong* in all things through him who strengthens me."

That's the message Paul is offering. Not that he can do all things and fulfill every dream. But that he continually celebrates the present and future fulfillment of God's restoration. And so he is content no matter his circumstances. He is strong in all things through the strength of Christ.

## BUILDING A BRIDGE TO YOUR RESTORATION

Here is another oft-quoted verse that, while not mistranslated, is often taken out of context.

> *"For I know the plans that I have for you," declares the Lord. "Plans for welfare and not for calamity to give you a future and a hope." (Jeremiah 29:11 NASB)*

This verse is typically offered to people living in the sorrow of lost dreams. And certainly, it is a comfort. God won't leave you where you are. He has a plan to restore you. But the comfort God offers isn't just about the future. He also suggests solutions for finding contentment in your present days.

It's important to look at the historical context this verse addresses. Jeremiah is speaking to those held captive as exiles in Babylon. Yes, he offers hope for Israel's eventual return to Jerusalem. But the return isn't going to happen for decades. And many hearing this comfort won't return to Jerusalem at all.

Verses that precede 29:11 give us a better sense of how Jeremiah expects them to understand this hope for restoration. While living in exile, he says they should:

> *Build houses and live in them; and plant gardens and eat their produce. Take wives and become the fathers of sons and daughters, and take wives for your sons and give your daughters to husbands, that they may bear sons and daughters; and multiply there and do not decrease. Seek the welfare of the city where I have sent you into exile, and pray to the Lord on its behalf; for in its welfare you will have welfare. (Jeremiah 29:5-7 NASB)*

Will God's plan for Israel's future include a return from exile?

Yes. But he doesn't want them to wait passively for this restoration. He wants them to take ownership of this hope by seeking the welfare of the city—by serving as agents of restoration in this place of exile and hopelessness. Despite them mourning their lost dreams, God isn't letting them off the hook. It is up to them to build a bridge to their restoration by assisting in that restoration from where they presently are.

## CONTENTMENT THROUGH A LIFE OF PROMISE

*All these died in faith, without receiving the promises; having seen them and having welcomed them from a distance; having confessed that they were strangers and exiles on the earth. (Hebrews 11:13 NASB)*

How should eternity shape your sense of contentment in the here-and-now? Is it enough to say your lost dreams don't matter compared to the rewards of heaven?

While you will experience poignant touches of the eternal while here on earth, the ultimate fulfillment of heavenly bliss is yet to come. And so the root of your present happiness must be grounded in the promise of eternity.

God indeed has a plan for your life. He has set before you a future worth having and a hope for more than you could ever imagine. But as an agent of his restoration, you yourself are part of the promise he's made to the world. So find your contentment by remaining faithful. And living a life of promise.

As you await the restoration of lost dreams, make the most of the life you've been given.

# PART V
# WEAKNESS CAN BE
# YOUR FUEL

Let's be honest. The journey of just one day can often wear us to the bone.

You start out with optimism and energy. You're going to tackle what needs doing with gusto!

Fifteen minutes later…that pipe dream is out the window.

Your spouse reminds you that you can't put off that errand any longer. Your kids mewl and cry like nursing kittens, needing to be fed or driven somewhere post-haste. The tasks awaiting you at your job plop on your chest with the sadistic pleasure of a schoolyard bully.

You trudge on through the day, bearing it the best you can. But when you lay down to sleep, there's nothing left. How can you keep this up even one more hour? What's the point of living if you don't have the strength to cope as it is?

That's just one simple day.

What about your journey unto life?

As each year passes into the next, we can find our souls as empty as a desert horizon. We wither under the strain of work and family. The demands to stay healthy and maintain a life of purpose feel more like a burden than a noble goal. All the while, we maintain the image of Christian strength when our spiritual tank is running on fumes.

If you identify with any of this...welcome to the club.

But understand: you're not suffering from a lack of fuel but from a lapse of memory. The memory that it was weakness that started you out on this journey—when you admitted your inability to master life and surrendered to God's saving grace. Again, the journey and the destination are one. The grace you began with is the same grace you'll need to make it to the end.

*My grace is sufficient for you, for power is perfected in weakness. (2 Corinthians 12:9 NASB)*

Your weakness, rather than being a reason to despair, is the key to moving forward in God's grace. In other words—weakness can be your fuel.

In these next reflections, you'll see how the good news of the Gospel isn't discovered by simply turning on some faith light switch to experience continual victory. It's found by accepting that the world (including you) still groans in the pain of suffering and sin.

Accepting this will give you access to a strength the world does not know.

And a fuel that will carry you to the finish line.

# THE RING OF TRUTH

In slumber, I sleep
In a stupor, I stoop
In the sacred, I soar

I once applied for a part-time job at the local zoo. I love animals. Some tell me I love animals more than people. That probably depends on the animal. Or the person.

Because I love animals, I debated whether working at a zoo wouldn't trouble my conscience. The jury's still out on this, but the fact that these creatures are raised outside their natural habitat does trouble me.

Our most common vision is of the large cat, be it a lion or leopard, pacing back and forth within his confines. Many zoos have larger, more organic environments than just cages. But you're still left to wonder—is this where they are meant to be?

I often find myself pacing like the lion. I push forward against the boundaries of my life, wishing I were somewhere else, learning to adapt inside my cage. I numb myself with processed food and television. I try to discipline myself to do the right thing. But I sometimes act when I shouldn't or don't act when I should. I more often sigh with resignation than roar with life.

But then in my stupor, I have the vaguest recollection that human cages are usually of our own making. Then I do something small, seemingly insignificant, and it all comes back to me.

Not long ago, I woke up deep inside my cage. I rose to go to work, buried underneath a landfill of wasteful anxiety—how was I going to solve the innumerable tasks the day held for me? I began to strategize, to push back against the fear, to breathe in and out and take one step forward.

It was early morning. As I wiped the condensation from my car, I raised my eyes to the pre-dawn sky. There, amid an expanse of darkest blue were a few orphan stars and the sliver of a moon. And my heart said, "Oh…"

ARE we like the caged animal? Are the bars of our own making? Do we, like John Donne once said, "neglect God and his angels for the noise of a fly, for the rattling of a coach, for the whining of a door"?[1] Where is our natural habitat? Is this where we are meant to be?

Maybe by a simple change of focus or a shift in location or activity, we'll move from the cage of our slumber or stupor into the realm of the sacred. The truth will finally ring true in our ears, and our heart will say, "Oh…"

Unlike the poor lion, most of our cage doors are already open.

It's a daily choice whether we'll step outside.

*One of the great sorrows which came to human beings when Adam and Eve left the garden was the loss of memory, memory of all that God's children are meant to be. — Madeleine L'Engle[2]*

# A BITTERSWEET SEASON

Like many, Christmas is by far my favorite time of year.
There is a richness of life and color. Houses, trees, and city
streets seem to stand up straighter as we all do when we put on
our best clothes. The world shines a pregnant glow. The air grows
cooler, and we imagine the warmth inside all those shops and
homes with smoke-filled chimneys.

We hear solemn and joyful music we only listen to once a
year. Even the most health-conscious among us tend to forego
our self-discipline for the rich banquets and sweet delicacies of
these waning, blissful days. And, of course, there is the joy of
family and friends, of giving and receiving, the joy of togetherness
that is more poignant than at any other time.

But accompanying this Norman Rockwell delight, others are
overwhelmed by a deep sadness. Perhaps because, while
reminded of the fullness of life and family, they instead find
exposed the empty spaces where that is missing for them, or at
least where it is stifled by the world's cruelty or human
dysfunction.

For years Christmas was a time of grief for my mom. Her own
mother died a few days before the holiday, so every year was a

reminder of that empty hole in her life. I remember when I was single how Christmas was about as bad as Valentine's Day. I didn't need another holiday to highlight how lonely I was.

There's so much self-inflicted stress during the holidays, with families trying to meet some unrealistic standard for the perfect gift, the perfect meal, or perfect gathering. But none of us are perfect, and Christmas often brings us front-and-center with that reality. Our blood pressure surges amid the press of extra traffic and crowded stores—so many people clamoring for togetherness they practically kill each other in its pursuit.

Again, Christmas is hard for many because we can't negotiate this nearness of the bitter with the sweet, with all we lack standing so close to this celebration of life. But I think that this is one of the chief opportunities in the season. The emptiness we feel can be a gateway to enjoying its richness.

Christmas celebrates the time when Jesus Christ, in all his glory and innocence, entered this world and came as close as you can get to our dysfunctional humanity and depravity. He was purposely conceived amid the sexual scandal of illegitimacy. The first news of his birth was given to shepherds, among the lowest social outcasts in that culture. He was born in the most impoverished conditions: without anesthetic, without medical assistance, amid animal waste and a complete lack of sanitation.

Christ's birth should never inspire a celebration that has no place for the things we lack. If anyone has cause to celebrate the season, it's the person who feels something is missing.

Christmas is a reminder that God is finally with us in our brokenness and longing—in our secret, selfish desires, our depression, our family fights; in our overeating, our obsession with giving the perfect gift, our grief over loved ones lost; in our aching desire for a spouse or a baby, in our desire to reconcile with that family member after so many years—God is now with us and can identify with our darkest existence.

Christ's arrival is meant to satisfy our yearning to know that we can come to God as we are, especially in all our melancholy hopelessness. This tiny, helpless child has come to let us hold him in our frail arms, to feel the warmth of his innocence, to experience a comfort that nurtures all that we are.

Christmas is for every one of us. Yes, for those who already know its joy, but also for those who don't.

It's all a little bittersweet. But I think that's the gift of the season.

# PAPIER-MÂCHÉ IDOLS

I have a real knack for self-delusion.

I was reminded of this recently when my wife and I spent some extended time outside the United States.[1] Having traveled internationally before, I told others I was the opposite of the Ugly American—I was adaptable to different cultures; I didn't need the trappings of first-world comfort to feel safe and secure.

Not long after arriving overseas, this self-image crumbled. I missed my favorite restaurants and access to US sporting events. I missed wide-laned highways and cultural norms that were instinctive and easy to follow. I missed conversations that didn't require constant translation. When we returned to the States, I breathed a sigh of relief. I was back where I belonged. I no longer had to feel the pain of my weakness and hypocrisy.

But upon our return, the seeds of my next phase of discomfort were already germinating in the remote regions of Asia. My hypocrisy reared its ugly head again with the coming of the Coronavirus health crisis.

Like all of us, I became homebound, robbed of creature comforts, convenience, and freedom. I missed my favorite restaurants and social gatherings. I was imprisoned inside dark thoughts and dire news headlines. I still had the stimulants of social media and digital entertainment, but these were exposed even more as the vacuous soul-nutrition they've always been.

## OUR GREATEST NEEDS

I've heard it said that the most fundamental human needs are *security* and *significance*. We all need security—shelter, food, health, and safety. But we also need significance—motivation, meaning, and purpose. Things like parenting and marriage give us significance. Most crave a satisfying vocation or career. We need to feel productive, that we're making a difference, that there's a reason we're here, and that we have a job that needs doing.

This global pandemic has attacked not just human bodies, but the human soul as well. It's attacked our sense of both security and significance. It's also awakened us to the tension between these two needs. Our survival instinct to secure ourselves and our families has been jutted against the significance that comes from living beyond just meeting our own desires and needs.

More critically, at least for me, the crisis has reminded me of yet another uncomfortable truth—I'm not as strong as I think I am. And many of the things I depend on for security and significance are not all they're cracked up to be.

But here's some good news. This loss of security and significance has opened up a window of opportunity.

## THE OPPORTUNITY IN LOSS

Here's a passage from my last book that may heighten this meaning.

> The opportunity in loss is that your choices become simpler, your focus more singular. When most everything is stripped from you, you can choose to despair, or you can choose to finally surrender

to the only one who can make things right. What you're really surrendering is your definition of what matters. You live on more than God, but God is all you ultimately need. Suffering loss is often the best gateway to this discovery.[2]

For many, the loss of health, loved ones, and livelihood has been devastating. For others (including me to this point), the loss of security and significance is far less, but no less eye-opening as an opportunity for growth. That opportunity will look different to each of us depending on the nature of our crisis and the differences within ourselves.

Some clues can be found, of course, from Jesus. He says, "What profit is it to a man if he gains the whole world and loses his own soul?"[3]

If we seek our strength through the world's security and significance but lose our soul, how strong will we be, really?

The strength of God and human strength (however imagined) cannot coexist within the same space. This rude awakening to weaknesses—my fear, my selfishness—could be a reason to despair. But it can also be the motivation I need to strip my false foundations and rebuild on something real and lasting: a revolution in my priorities; laying siege to my papier-mâché idols; a re-commitment to trust in God's wisdom, love, and provision regardless of whether my life is going according to plan.

In the loss of self-reliance, I discover my true self or who I'm meant to be. In the loss of self-delusion, I discover the life God wants me to live.

## SHALL WE OVERCOME?

My wife and I took a hike the other day and found ourselves so refreshed. After isolating in the house due to Covid, we were thrilled to breathe in the deep source of oxygen provided by close-knit foliage and trees. We drank in the beauty and sustenance of God's created world.

But as we struggled up and down different inclines, I realized the greatest benefit from the hike was the opportunity to overcome an obstacle outside myself. It was a break from focusing just on my internal, futile battle to overcome.

I'm not as strong as I think I am. I feel as selfish and fearful and helpless as anyone during this season. Perhaps the only strategy I've learned is to move beyond the crisis occurring between my two ears and seek rescue from something—or *someone*—outside myself. To learn from this loss and exchange my weakness for God's strength.

The pandemic isn't over yet so I imagine new lessons will arise.

My life here on earth isn't over either. As long as I'm breathing, I have some growing to do. I have work to do.

And so do you.

# SPEAKING TRUTH TO POWER

Who was this man?

Pontius Pilate stared at Jesus. Dressed in the attire of the common poor, he was brought to Pilate bound, disheveled, bruised from some recent beating. He wasn't much to look at, to be sure. But he'd been accused of insurrection against Rome. And so, as Rome's authority in the region, it was up to Pilate to question him.

"Are You the King of the Jews?"

Jesus answered, "My kingdom is not of this world. If my kingdom were of this world, then my servants would be fighting so that I would not be handed over to the Jews."

"So, you are a king?"

Jesus said, "You say correctly that I am a king. For this, I have been born, and for this I have come into the world, to testify to the truth. Everyone who is of the truth hears my voice."

Pilate said to him, "What is truth?"[1]

For Pilate, in the seat of Rome's supreme power, there would be no answer. In perhaps the peak of history's dramatic irony, there was no need to answer—because truth was staring him right in the face. But he couldn't see it. And so goes the story of truth's relationship to power.

MOST MODERN JOURNALISTS define their mission as "speaking truth to power." They're charged with holding those in power accountable by bringing the truth about their dealings into the light of day. This mission has also been championed by many minorities and those fighting for civil rights. The objective of speaking the truth is to keep power in check. To stop or at least minimize the potential for tyranny over others.

But the desire for power holds sway over more than just politicians or corporate monopolies. It affects us all and permeates every pore of society and human consciousness.

Consider just a few headlines of the day. The debate concerning gun violence and gun control, for example. Isn't this a debate about power? The power to keep society safe versus the power to retain personal freedoms and self-protection. Or the "#MeToo" movement. This is about standing up against the abuse of power through sexual harassment and assault. Within most of today's headlines, you'll discover a constant struggle for power.

Blockbuster movies feature heroes fighting evil with their superpowers. Most sports celebrate overpowering an opponent. We cling to news updates on the stock market and the economy. Will we remain empowered to live the quality of life we deserve?

And, of course, back to politics. We're obsessed with who's in power, most often at the national level. And too many have become either blind followers or mockers, depending on who's in power at the time. Party has become more important than principle, and the truths we say we care about are compromised in the name of holding onto, or regaining, power.

Our desire for power is so pervasive that many would side with the philosopher Friedrich Nietzsche in saying that throughout history, there's never been any universal truth at all, but only creeds designed to overpower, fabricated by those in places of power. Sadly, this has indeed been the case with many human claims of truth. But does that mean there's no truth to be found in the divine?

"What is truth?"

Asking that question may have been Pilate's most truthful moment. As someone in a place of power, his chief objective wasn't truth, it was not losing the power he had. There he was, face-to-face with perhaps the most powerless-looking man he'd ever known, who would soon experience the height of powerlessness through a brutal torture and death. But again, within this powerless man, divine truth was there for anyone with eyes to see.

## AT THE FOOT OF THE CROSS

The evangelist Billy Graham was once traveling in a golf cart through a football stadium with a local mayor. Tens of thousands of fans cheered for him. But Graham was embarrassed: "I think they're confused. This is not about me."[2]

Billy Graham understood the truth when he saw it. He was often quoted as saying that the ground is level at the foot of the cross. He had no taste for the power of his world-renowned reputation. He gave all credit to Jesus Christ, who didn't come to be served, but to serve, and to give his life as a ransom for many.

What is the truth? We love to hold others to account, but can we speak truth to our own power? The instinct is understandable. We crave control over our lives. We want the freedom to live as we wish. We want to keep ourselves safe. And we want to stand up to those who would overpower us for their own gain.

But what is the truth? The truth is, in our desire to pursue, retain, and defend power, we're chasing a mirage that always promises but never delivers. Power is indeed the key to enjoying a life of spiritual fulfillment, but it is not the power within we need, but power from on high. And as the life and death of Jesus demonstrates, power from on high is only received through the embrace of powerlessness—through the person who surrenders control of their life to God.

You should never stop speaking truth to the powers-that-be when they become corrupt. And you should never stop standing up to those who would abuse you if you've been affected by injustice, racial prejudice, sexual assault, or even death.

But while seeking to overcome such tyranny, make sure you speak your truths at the foot of the cross: where weakness discovers strength, where the humble are exalted, where the poor in spirit rest in heaven's kingdom. Surrender yourself to the empowered powerlessness of Christ, lay down your life for those still held captive by their own power, and you'll find a life beyond imagining.

Where, like Jesus standing resolutely before Pilate, even the power of death can hold no sway over your heart and mind.

*Do you not know? Have you not heard? The everlasting God, the Lord, the Creator of the ends of the earth does not become weary or tired…He gives strength to the weary, and to him who lacks might he increases power. Though youths grow weary and tired, and vigorous young men stumble badly, yet those who wait for the Lord will gain new strength. They will mount up with wings like eagles, they will run and not get tired, they will walk and not become weary. (Isaiah 40:28-31 NASB)*

*For yours is the kingdom and the power and the glory forever. Amen. (Matthew 6:13 NASB)*

# PART VI
# TRAVELING COMPANIONS ARE YOUR "WHY"

I assume you've heard of thru-hikers?

These are hikers who don't just take a short stroll through the woods or head out for just one day. They walk much longer distances, sometimes thousands of miles, like along the Appalachian or Pacific Crest trails. These hikes can last for many months.

Why do they hike so far? And how do they make it to the end? You'll hear different answers, depending on the hiker. But most will tell you that a big reason they went the distance, a big reason they return to hike similar journeys—are their traveling companions. The folks they hiked with or met along the way.

As you'd expect, thru-hikers often lose the stamina to keep going. They experience pain, exhaustion, and loneliness. But a known companion or those they meet on the trail will encourage them to keep going. And likewise, they help others move forward, too. The burden of any journey is lessened when shared.

Now, on the flip side, fellow hikers can also be troublesome. Some may want to travel at a different pace. Some may want to stop, go back, or choose another way. Some personalities are just not a fit. The more time spent with other hikers, the harder it can be to get along. However, in looking back, many realize this wasn't a hindrance to their journey. These conflicts played an important role in the journey, too.

The Holocaust-survivor, Viktor Frankl, quoting Nietzsche, said, "He who has a 'why' to live for can bear almost any 'how.'"[1] In your journey unto life, traveling companions are often your "why."

Jesus said:

> Love one another, even as I have loved you...By this all men will know that you are my disciples, if you have love for one another. (John 13:34-35 NASB)

Our very identity as Jesus' disciples is found in how well we love one another. Learning to love others well—both in times of harmony and conflict—defines the journey itself. It's the reason we walk at all.

These next reflections explore the challenges and rewards of journeying with others—the power in small acts of kindness, the pain we inflict and endure, the liberation that comes from grace, and how true belonging can only be enjoyed through Christ's greatest act of love.

Make no mistake. The trail before you is long. So don't walk it alone.

The journey isn't meant just for you.

# THE MIRACLE OF A SIMPLE GREETING

From the very beginning, God said, "It is not good that man should be alone."[1] But so often, we are alone. We isolate inside houses and fenced-in yards. We abandon real human interaction for our smartphones, social media, and cable news. We cut ourselves off from the life-affirming purpose found in serving our neighbor with humility and grace.

How can we break down these walls? It can begin in the simplest way.

Put down your smartphone and step outside the door. Walk the sidewalks in your neighborhood or along the aisles in Walmart. Observe the people around you. You'll see the isolation. Faces hardened. Distracted. Carrying the weight of the world.

Then say something like, "Hello! How are you today?" Or, "Hi. My name's _____. How's your day been going?"

It's just a simple greeting. But when I've done this, I've often been floored by the results. In the twinkling of an eye, the fortress is gone. Their expression softens. Some laugh in stunned surprise. Some return the greeting and offer me their name. A few share their troubles with a perfect stranger, taking advantage that someone actually cares they exist.

It's such an easy thing to do. But it produces a miracle. A resurrection from the grave of aloneness and isolation. And it makes me wonder: if just one greeting can do this, what could more human interaction do?

A life rule I try to live by is this:

*Be kind—for everyone you meet is fighting a great battle.*[2]

Whether they acknowledge it or not, no matter how annoying or offensive they are, everyone is fighting a great battle. And most are fighting it alone.

Jesus said, "Love one another just as I have loved you. Greater love has no one than this, that one lay down his life for his friends."[3]

How did Jesus love others? He laid down his life. Ultimately, by dying on the cross. But whether it was convenient or not, he also showed kindness to those fighting great battles. He loved the whole world, especially those whom his tribe considered foreign, unacceptable, a corrupting influence on society. Jesus didn't have to agree with someone's beliefs or behavior before treating them with kindness. He laid down his life to love those in need.

One of those "unacceptables"—Mary Magdalene—once stood alone outside an empty tomb on Easter morning, in tears that someone had taken away her Lord.

Jesus approached her, but she didn't recognize him until he offered her a greeting.

He said, "Mary."

It was just a simple greeting. But as she clung to her risen Lord, it was as though she had risen, too.

She knew she was no longer alone.

## THROWING IN THE TOWEL

Throughout my younger years, I was often the victim of bullying. It took different forms, but usually involved verbal name-calling and teasing.

The teasing led to perhaps the most traumatic season of my life. I was ready to quit school and hide in my bedroom 'till I was eighteen. Finally at their wits' end, my parents sent me to see a counselor. There, the counselor addressed my responsibility in the situation—how I reacted to the teasing.

He brought out a large bath towel and asked me to grab onto one end as he took hold of the other. At his urging, we both started to pull and entered a tug-of-war. On his side, he said he'd play the role of my peers, and so he started calling me names: "Stupid, idiot, geek!" He asked me to respond the best I could: "I'm not an idiot! I'm smart! I'm not a geek!"

The tension rose. I pulled with all my might, but he was much bigger and it was all I could do to hold on.

Then he startled me with an insane request:

"Let go."

Why would he say that? I was doing what he'd asked me to do. It made no sense.

My emotions surged. I thought, *I can't let go. I'll lose! I'll be giving in! If I let go, I'll become what they say I am.*

He said it again: "Let go."

I couldn't do it. My survival felt at stake. Letting go meant falling backward into?...I didn't know. I thought it might be the end of me.

Finally, he yelled at the top of his lungs:

"Let go!!!!!"

So, I let go. I stumbled backward, nearly falling to the floor. We were both out of breath, sweating from the tug-of-war.

Now, I don't remember exactly what he said next. But the gist was something like this:

> "Where is the problem now? By letting go of the struggle, not defending yourself so stridently, you've left no fuel for their fire. But by continuing to hold on, it is you who contributes to your own demise."

ONCE I ENTERED HIGH SCHOOL, I grew more self-confident, better realizing my gifts, building my self-esteem. Yet I've never broken completely free from the effects of that teasing.

A few years ago I was in a minivan with my 11-year-old nephew sitting right behind me. He started messing around, kicking the seat, pulling my hair, laughing at me. I did my best to behave like an adult uncle and asked him to stop. But a pang of helplessness surfaced inside me. It was something I hadn't felt in years. I was back in the 7th grade all over again.

However, while I still struggle in this area, I understand I don't always need to defend my honor when I feel judged by others. My most important source of worth comes from God— what others think of me doesn't mean much in the greater scheme of things.

Can you identify? When someone opposes us, we pull and pull on our towel—we're so weary from the effort, but fear that letting go might somehow be the end of us.

However, God wants our relationships to be more proactive than reactive. There is freedom in focusing less on what someone is doing to us and more on what we can do for them. When we release ourselves from the struggle and instead offer grace, we get the peace we've always wanted, but never knew how to find.

Whether it's hurtful comments from a friend, a family argument, or any area of conflict—we can give up our need to be right. We can turn the other cheek and lay down our lives for the sake of another. When we do, we'll become a bit more like Jesus, whose own response to unjust treatment showed us the path to true freedom, self-worth, and love.

So don't be surprised if in the midst of your next human tug-of-war, God interrupts you with this insane request:

*Let go. Throw in the towel!*

Despite your best instincts, that's how you'll win the fight.

# FREEDOM IN RELATIONSHIP

J ean Valjean was "a dangerous man."

That was the description of him written on the yellow passport he carried. After nineteen years of imprisonment for the crime of stealing a loaf of bread, he was set free. But although now outside the prison walls, he knew he was still a prisoner. The passport proved this to all he encountered.

Arriving at a village, he stopped at an inn, but as an ex-convict, he was barred from entering. Children then followed him down the street, throwing stones. Even the local jailer rejected him, saying he'd need to be arrested again to find any lodging there. To his astonishment, he was finally received by the local bishop who gave him hot food and a warm place to sleep.

But even after this kindness, Valjean was no less hardened. His long imprisonment had sealed his hatred and mistrust. So, in the middle of the night, he left, after stealing the bishop's precious silverware.

In the morning, the bishop answered his door to find Valjean bound in chains, in the custody of the local police who had caught him with the stolen silver. Breaking the terms of his parole, he would be sent back to prison—this time, for life.

"Ah, here you are!" said the bishop, looking toward Jean Valjean.
"'I am glad to see you. But how is this? I gave you the candle-
sticks too, which are silver like the rest, for which you can
certainly get two hundred francs. Why did you not take them
along with your forks and spoons?"

Jean Valjean opened his eyes wide and stared at the bishop
with an expression no human tongue could render any account of.

As the police released him and left, Valjean felt like a man just
about to faint.

The bishop drew near to him and said in a low voice, "Do not
forget, never forget that you have promised to use this money in
becoming an honest man."

Jean Valjean, who had no recollection of ever having promised
anything, remained speechless. The bishop emphasized the words
when he uttered them. He resumed with solemnity:

"Jean Valjean, my brother, you no longer belong to evil, but to
good. It is your soul that I buy from you. I withdraw it from black
thoughts and the spirit of perdition, and I give it to God."[1]

THE STORY of Jean Valjean explores the drama of human
bondage and freedom.

We who live in western democracies celebrate freedom as a
way of life. We are free to worship, we're free to speak our minds,
to live where we like. But Valjean knew there was more to
freedom than just our civil liberties. Other tyrannies can imprison
us: prejudice, hatred, selfishness, guilt, depression, recklessness.
In the eyes of others we may appear free, but like Valjean, we may
still walk in hopeless bondage.

A young child might be teased in the schoolyard, a woman
could suffer years of abuse from her husband, a qualified man

may be passed over repeatedly for a promotion because of the color of his skin. Our world can be cruel, and often due to circumstances beyond our control, we find ourselves trapped in prisons from which we cannot escape.

Sometimes the bondage is of our own making. However unjust, Jean Valjean understood his years in prison were the consequence of his own actions. Freedom involves not just the ability to choose, but where our choices take us. A man may be free to drink as much alcohol as he likes, but if his drinking leads to addiction, unemployment, divorce, a lost and lonely life, perhaps even death—how free is he in his freedom?

We are only truly free when our choices are guided by more than just what we want for ourselves. This harkens back to the principle I've mentioned in other writings, that *life is relationship.* If our purpose is founded on our most important relationships, then true freedom can only be enjoyed by making our independence subject to the expectations of those relationships.

For most of us, this lesson is best learned through our encounters with God and those who serve him. We're compelled to live differently after experiencing God's undeserved grace.

Jean Valjean was a hard man, rejected and forgotten by most of society. The bishop not only welcomed him with food and rest but also offered him a reprieve from prison and the wealth of silver to start his life anew. Shocked by this grace, Valjean was now compelled to live his life for others—because of a freedom received that he in no way deserved.

As followers of Jesus Christ, we're offered this same freedom.

*There is now no condemnation for those who are in Christ Jesus. For the law of the Spirit of life in Christ Jesus has set you free from the law of sin and of death. (Romans 8:1-2 NASB)*

Freedom was one of the main objectives of Jesus' mission here on earth. He came to "proclaim freedom for the prisoners...to set the oppressed free."[2] He restored relationships, he fed the hungry, he healed the sick. Jesus freed people to live beyond their own selfish choices so they could enjoy life to the full.

This is the liberty God wants for us all. Yes, he wants us to be free from all that binds us. But he ultimately wants us to be free *for* one another. Like the moment you commit to your spouse in marriage only to find the freedom that comes from love and family, God wants us to surrender ourselves to his love and commit our lives to following him.

There is freedom within the bonds of godly relationship. The bishop had been liberated by Christ's love and therefore liberated Valjean. Freed from his bitterness and hatred, Valjean then devoted his life to doing good and helping the poor and the vulnerable. Freely he received. Freely he gave.

What about you and me?

If we've also been liberated by grace, what will we choose to do with it?

*Is this not the fast which I choose—to loosen the bonds of wickedness, to undo the bands of the yoke, to let the oppressed go free and break every yoke? Is it not to divide your bread with the hungry and bring the homeless poor into the house? When you see the naked, to cover him? And not to hide yourself from your own flesh?*

*If you remove the yoke from your midst, the pointing of the finger and speaking wickedness, if you give yourself to the hungry and satisfy the desire of the afflicted, then your light will rise in darkness and your gloom will become like midday. The Lord will continually guide you, satisfy your desire in scorched places, and give strength to your bones. You will be like a watered garden, like a spring of water whose waters do not fail. (Isaiah 58:6-7,9-11 NASB)*

# BETWEEN KEITH AND THE NUNS

There is a mystery to belonging.

I'm reminded of this early on Sunday mornings.

I bought an alarm clock that allows you to wake up to the music of your choice rather than some annoying radio station or a loud buzzer.

My wife and I have a mix of songs that begin our morning with a heart of worship—this helps our attitude as we start the day. The first tune is an all-time favorite: *Easter Song* by Keith Green, celebrating the resurrection of Jesus Christ.

We always enjoy hearing this song, but on Sunday mornings, it means a bit more. It begins a time together that is just our own —no job to worry about, no television, no friends or family, no phone calls, no social media—just my wife and I, waking up together, talking and enjoying each other without distraction.

There's a visceral sense of peace and belonging that feels uniquely ours during that time. And most often, it doesn't matter if we had a big argument the night before, whether I was an insensitive jerk or she was critical or anxious. When we hear Keith's piano bursting through the web of our fitful dreams, we remember a mercy that's renewed with the morning and the value of unconditional acceptance and intimacy. It's the time, more than any other, when I feel the most married.

A few songs later, the nuns from the musical *The Sound of Music* invoke a glorious welcome to the industry of the day. This is our reminder that it's time to get out of bed if we're going to make it to church on time. We both usually groan, not wanting to rise, but also for the end of those fleeting moments.

Sure, we could set the alarm to go off earlier, which we have. Sure, I could create other moments of quiet and intimacy, which I do. But for now, this has been our pattern. And because it's this temporary moment of grace, it feels all the more precious to both of us.

MY WIFE and I have been working with married couples for several years, and next week, I'll be starting a new class on marriage at our church. While it's just an arbitrary matter of scheduling, the class will begin the day after Easter. So right now I have marriage on my mind as much as I have the suffering and resurrection of Christ.

I'm wondering whether that's a coincidence.

Why? Because marriage is perhaps my best daily reminder of the suffering and resurrection Jesus experienced for our sakes.

Paul said of him:

*I want to know Christ—to know the power of his resurrection and participation in his sufferings. Becoming like him in his death and so somehow attaining to the resurrection from the dead. (Philippians 3:10-11 NIV)*

We sometimes make jokes about the ancient phrasing in the Bible where Adam "knowing" his wife is a polite euphemism for sexual relations. And while it is perhaps just that, I think it also means a great deal more.

There's more to a healthy marriage than just carnal knowledge or sexual union. There's intimacy in the realm of the intellect, the emotions, and ultimately, in the realm of the spiritual. Two become one in a mysterious one-flesh relationship. In this way, marriage is related to the way we can know Christ—a communion that includes every part of who we are.

As Paul notes above, knowing Christ fully means sharing in both his crucifixion and his resurrection. This intimate, new life in Christ can't be enjoyed without first participating in his suffering and death.

And so it is with marriage. When you get married, you can't hide your selfishness any longer. It shows up in spades after you say your vows. Therefore, the only way to have a marriage of happiness and true belonging—to truly know that person physically, emotionally, spiritually—you must die to the selfish desire to always go your own way.

My wife and I have felt this many times. It hurts to let go of what I want. It feels like a death. I've spent ample time mourning the loss of my own way. But no matter how justified I've felt in standing up for the conviction that I'm right, if it means we don't speak to each other and live separately under the same roof, then all I am is *dead* right. Without her, I have no life worth living.

So, to experience resurrection life in my marriage, I have to give myself up.

> *Husbands, love your wives, just as Christ loved the church and gave himself up for her... "For this reason a man will leave his father and mother and be united to his wife, and the two will become one flesh." This is a profound mystery—but I am talking about Christ and the church. (Ephesians 5:25,31-32 NIV)*

There's the connection. Husband to wife. Christ to the church.

We all want to be accepted. We all want to belong. But most

often, a price must be paid for our acceptance. Christ paid that price over 2,000 years ago so we could belong to God. And through his power and guidance, my wife and I experience this mystery as well. Despite our innumerable weaknesses, she accepts me and I accept her.

So, it's no accident that some of the most precious times in my marriage are accompanied by a song about new life and the Easter resurrection. Each Sunday, this mercy is renewed with the dawn and I'm reminded of the price paid for our acceptance—both when my wife and I put each other's needs above our own, and when Jesus put the needs of the world above his right to life itself.

No. I don't think it's a coincidence. There is a link between marriage and Holy Week.

With me and my wife, the link is discovered between Keith and the nuns, and it will last so long as we both shall live.

With Christ and his bride, the marriage will never end.

# PART VII
# WHEN GOD'S PATH BECOMES YOURS

Not everything in your journey is about traveling directly from point A to point B.

We imagine our life as a straightforward path. It starts somewhere and has a finish line. And to reach our goal we only have to move in one direction.

But while there is a start and finish to your earthly journey, it often involves anything but straightforward movement. There are obstacles you must navigate, climb over, or go around. You'll hit roadblocks and detours. Delays can postpone your movement by days, weeks, or years. You may get lost and have to return to the point you first went astray.

But in looking back over where you've been, you'll likely find the crooked path wasn't by accident. Even if some of it was caused by your misjudgments or failures, you realize God still had a plan. He either ordained your choices or used them for your eternal good and the good of others. Humbled that you ever tried to follow your own way, your perspective finally aligns with his—God's path becomes yours.

These next reflections detail one chapter in my own journey of directed misdirection. Many years ago, my path became more focused when I entered seminary to serve God's people through writing, teaching, and pastoral ministry. That dream was fulfilled in many ways, but it seemed never more so than when I was called to pastor a church in the country of Honduras.

I haven't written about my time serving there, but of my thoughts just before and after. As they are some of my most personal and vulnerable writings to date, I debated whether to include them in this book. But I do so for the same reasons I wrote them down in the first place.

To model the path unto life for others, we must show both the good and the bad. The good, so they can see why it's worth following. But also the bad, or challenging, so they can see that this journey is accessible to all, especially those who don't think they can do it.

Jesus' earthly journey also included roadblocks and detours. While ultimately victorious, it was first filled with weakness, humiliation, and suffering. And while he never strayed from God's path, he still "learned obedience from the things he suffered."[1] So, Jesus is sympathetic to our challenges, but he's also a beacon of hope that we can keep returning to God's path and join him at the finish line.

Like me, your path has probably included serving others—your family, your church, your community, or those beyond the boundaries of your culture or nation. When it has, you've probably, like me, found yourself moving one step forward and two steps back. Stumbling along the way, you may lose confidence that you can follow God's path at all.

But this shouldn't stop you from running toward each new adventure when he calls you to serve. Remember—in your journey unto life, God works all things together for good, for those who love him and are called according to his purpose.[2]

# A STRANGER IN A LAND OF
# PROMISE

I was in the mountains.

In these mountains, I knew I belonged. I was at peace, but not ready to retire. I was full of anticipation, but the unknowns now felt like a gift.

This time though, I wasn't in the mountains of North Carolina. I was in the Central American country of Honduras—where God was calling me and my wife to serve.

How did I get there?

That's a story worth telling.

Not long ago, I sent an email to a church in search of a new pastor. They had been praying for a pastor for some time and were eager for God to answer. The church is an English-speaking congregation mostly filled with *expatriates*: North American citizens who've come to work in the country as missionaries, school teachers, embassy employees, and so on.

While I've had a "one day" dream to pastor a church, I had no desire to do it any time soon and certainly not in Honduras. My wife and I found our dream home in the Smokies and had no plans to move. I had no real knowledge of Honduras other than its location somewhere south of the United States. Yet one

Sunday morning, I remembered the church's advertisement and felt a strong burden to start a conversation.

The opening lines of my first communication said, "I'm not sure I should even be sending you this email..."

Why? Because we'd found our dream home. Because I'd moved to the Smoky Mountains to serve in retreat ministry. Because I wasn't a traditional "CEO," "Type A" leader. Because I was a sinner. Because I was sometimes too sensitive to the judgment that comes with pastoring. Because, because, because...

But I still felt the burden, saying to myself, *if God's calling me there, he'll open the doors to make it happen.* This started a long application process where, to my stunned surprise, I kept advancing through each stage of elimination. As I advanced, I became more serious about my discernment process. I read Scripture and books on pastoral vocation. I prayed and sought advice from wise counselors. Despite my concerns, I still believed in the calling of God. If God made his calling clear, no excuses could justify my disobedience.

Of course, there were also many reasons in favor of applying. I've long recognized my vocation as a teacher and communicator of God's Word. Despite my introverted leanings, I've always been drawn to life-changing personal encounters with other human beings. And my life has been most blessed when playing an active role in healthy, growing Christian communities.

Since moving to North Carolina, doors for such service have been closed for me. And in God's purposes, closed doors often mean he's opening doors elsewhere. But Central America?

In the Bible, Abraham is called to a place unknown where God will bless him and make him a blessing. In the foreign land of Canaan, he is called "a stranger in the land of promise."[1] As my application proceeded, it became apparent God was issuing similar marching orders. The church chose me as their final candidate and my wife and I were flown down to see Honduras firsthand. I preached a sermon and received a final vote of approval from the congregation.

So beyond all my expectations, it has happened. A church has called me to pastor.

And not just a church, but a church full of ministers. And not just an American church, but a church in a foreign land. A land with mountains like the Appalachians. Marked by immense poverty, but also by an unbending creativity for survival. A land full of both danger and gentle hospitality. A land of deeply-rooted culture, organic foods, and organic living. A land full of political unrest, brokenness, loneliness, and spiritual bondage—but a land full of promise. A place where I'm a stranger, but where God's redemptive hand is no stranger at all.

In so many ways, pastoring a church feels beyond me. But in these months of discernment, I've seen through one confirmation after another that, while beyond *me*, the calling is full of God.

And while this vocation comes with a weighty charge and responsibility, I know I'll be most useful not by taking charge, but by allowing myself to be used for God's glory—according to his will and his ways.

So, whether north or south, God still has me in the mountains. I look out over his heavenly expanse and am in awe of what awaits.

In awe, but no longer afraid.

# THE THINGS WE LEAVE BEHIND

T he beauty of God's eternal plan remains untouched by my worldly
cares.

That phrase meanders through my brain as I look out from
our porch this morning. The North Carolina ridges stretch lazily
in their Sabbath repose. The clouds stroll merrily by. The
morning sun highlights the firmament with brushstrokes of
praise. Creation moves on in supreme procession while I
whimper away with these tiresome thoughts, bowing to the god
of petty anxiety.

Inside the house, we've been negotiating what to take with us
to Honduras and what to leave behind. There's no right or wrong
here necessarily. For us, it seems wiser to leave most of what we
own behind and start fresh after we arrive. My wife is no more
materialistic than me, but our home is her craftwork, her artistic
expression of love, family, and hospitality. Letting go isn't easy.

And yet Jesus pesters with this reminder...

*Your life does not consist in the abundance of your possessions.* [1]

Sure, that's good to know. But my stress lies less in the loss of things than in their management. Selling cars, houses, and other items has left me with little energy and optimism for what lies ahead. Why do we own all this stuff? Will we have enough money for what we need? Will our house remain on the market for years? How will we protect our future livelihood and well-being?

A cardinal dances on a branch near my porch. He pays me no mind. He hops. He flips upside down. He looks left with a jerk. Then right. He has no idea what a mortgage is and wouldn't know what to do with one if he did.

Jesus speaks again...

*Look at the birds of the air: they neither sow nor reap nor gather into barns, and yet your heavenly Father feeds them. Are you not of more value than they?*[2]

Yes, of course. God cares for everything he's created. But if I'm being honest, even greater anxiety comes with pastoring my first church. I'm exposing myself to criticism, judgment, and rejection. I've been safe within these Smoky Mountains. Safe from judgment. But also safe from making any real difference in the lives of others.

Jesus now clears his throat ("ahem!") and shares this pesky little truth...

*If anyone would come after me, let him deny himself and take up his cross and follow me. For whoever would save his life will lose it, but whoever loses his life for my sake will find it.*[3]

I look out at the view again. How safe are the Smokies, really? Storms can invade with violent winds and the deluge of rain. But the winds then die, waters recede, and the world returns to a place of wholeness. Who am I to understand these cycles of upheaval and restoration?

An old hymn writer whispers...

*Whatever the Lord pleases, he does—in heaven and on earth, in the seas and all deeps. It's he who makes the clouds rise at the end of the earth, who makes lightning for the rain and brings forth the wind from his storehouses.*[4]

So, what am I truly leaving behind? Perhaps it's my illusion of ownership and control. I don't imagine for one second I own the mountains I see before me. Or the clouds. Or the morning light. These are owned by God. Why do I imagine I even own this house? Or this furniture? Or this car?

Why do I think that as one of God's created works I own my very life? Isn't it possible my anxiety is rooted in some naive illusion that I have control over anything?

What if I were to leave behind my plans and offer everything up to God's plan? Won't God guide me and feed me? Won't he sustain me through any storms of loss and rejection? Won't God heal and restore?

An ancient pastor with some experience in these matters is bursting to chime in…

*Not that I have already obtained it or am already perfect, but I press on to make it my own because Christ Jesus has made me his own.*[5]

I'm not perfect. That's a certainty. I'm one holy mess who God in his unfathomable wisdom has assigned to care for his people. But I can still press on into God's plan. Because as a created being, I'm no different than that contented cardinal, these resting hills, the playful clouds, this glorious morning light. They are his and I am his. The main truth I need to grasp is this—that I am his.

So, I take a deep breath and mimic the hills in their Sabbath repose. Returning to the view before me, I echo a prayer from a past theologian.

God, I thank you for this universe, our great
home; for its vastness and its riches, and
for the manifold life which teems upon it
and of which we are part.

I praise you for the arching sky and the
blessed winds, for the driving clouds and
the constellations on high.

I praise you for the salt sea and the running
water, for the everlasting hills, for the
trees, and for the grass under our feet.

I thank you for our senses by which we can
see the splendor of the morning, and hear
the jubilant songs of love, and smell the
breath of springtime.

I pray that you'd give us a heart wide open to
all this joy and beauty and save our souls
from being so steeped in care or so dark-
ened by passion that we pass heedless and
unseeing when even the thorn bush by
the way is aflame with the glory of God.[6]

What he said.

Amen.

# I'VE COME HERE TO BE

Happy New Year, dear reader.

While it may seem like I'm writing again due to some New Year's resolution, it's just coincidental to other circumstances. We recently landed back on US soil and have settled for now in Virginia. We've been here long enough that I can focus on moving forward. And moving forward includes writing again.

Why have you not heard from me since we left for Honduras? The easiest answer is laziness. But I also have a compartmental temperament. When faced with a serious task, I choose whenever possible to focus solely on that task. So, for the most part, while serving the church in Honduras, that's all I did.

I'm not certain how much reflection I'll offer on my time there, at least for the moment. It was a deeply fruitful and challenging season—more challenging due to my deep-seated insecurities than due to the location or the people. I shouldn't devalue the gift in those challenges, so I will likely write more on them in the near future.

I will disclose that I'll always treasure the native people of Honduras: their richness of heart, their bright spirit in serving others, their absolute flexibility and creativity to take what has been given them and live life to the full. I'll also remember the wonderful church where we served. There is a fusion of generosity and fortitude in that community I've found unmatched in many other churches.

I return to the States humbled and a bit "in limbo" to be honest with you. I'm not sure what's ahead. My wife, for reasons surpassing reason, continues to follow me wherever I go. She's a miracle walking—always in love with wherever she lives, finding instant community with whomever she meets. To say I don't deserve her is a profound understatement.


## BETWEEN TWO STRAIGHT CREEKS

As mentioned, we're presently staked in Virginia, to be more specific, in Highland County and the town of Monterey. Founded before the Civil War, this town of 200 (once known as *Bell's Place*) was first described as "a patch of woods and laurel thickets on the saddle between two straight creeks." It has since grown, but thankfully not by much.

I hesitate to describe it in detail as we've just arrived. It feels like I must earn my credentials to write about it by living here a while. I will say though that photos and video don't compare to seeing it in person, even in this leafless winter season. Called Virginia's *Little Switzerland*, the area does have that feel with valleyed hamlets and roaming flocks of sheep and cattle.

But the Swiss allusion should only be what gets you here. Once here, you'll find it deserves its own demarcation. More than an hour from interstates and dissonant commerce, it has in some ways an *out west* feel, away from the things of man. And yet it still boasts a thriving and active community that belies its small and isolated population.

Everyone we've met so far has been welcoming. Although I've

been told we will be seen as *Come Heres* by the *Been Heres*—some with generational links spanning back near the birth of our country. But I've also been told that many *Come Heres* have been here for several decades now and may soon be equal in number to the *Been Heres*.

Most of us *Come Heres* are here for a reason. We don't want to change things. We're here to detach from the virtual and national and attach to what's local and real. To embrace the slow, the organic, the grounding effect of the difficult and inconvenient. To think and live life firsthand again, or in some ways, for the very first time.

I hesitate to wax too poetic about my own specific goals in this pursuit, even though I have many. I've done that in past writings and didn't live up to everything I set out to do. For now I'll just say that I'm still moving forward and haven't given up satisfying my ache for resonant and authentic living. And so while I may journal my progress, I do want to be more a student right now than teacher.

## WENDELL BERRY

In that light, I'm immersing myself in the writings of Kentucky naturalist, Wendell Berry. I've put off reading Berry for some time, mostly because so many I knew spoke of him in almost worshipful tones. I tend to resist the latest cultural trend or what's considered cool. But I believe most of the *Come Heres* of Highland County have come here because they share at least some of Berry's naturalistic vision for living.

And while I feel far from his earned intimacy with the soil and creation, I do think Berry's language and heart are linked with mine. So I'll be sitting at his feet a while amid these ancient mountains, valleys, and streams.

In his essay, *Native Hill*, Berry writes:

My mind is never empty or idle at the joining of streams. Here is the work of the world going on. The creation is felt, alive and intent on its materials in such places. In the angle of the meeting of two streams stands the steep wooded point of the ridge, like the prow of an upturned boat—finished as it was a thousand years ago, as it will be in a thousand years. Its becoming is only incidental to its being. It will be because it is. It has no aim or end except to be. By being, it is growing and wearing into what it will be.[1]

I agree with the idea, so present in Berry's writings, that we can often uncover the universal and eternal by paying attention to the God-made particular. In this case, by apprenticing ourselves under the frameless supervision of the natural, created world.

Unlike Berry's stream-formed ridge, I too often micromanage what I'm becoming—morally, spiritually (that was a recurring struggle for me in Honduras.) But if my supernatural being is in any way consistent with God's natural world, I should understand that what I'm becoming is only incidental to what God has made me to be.

As God in his great wisdom has created me to be *something*, then maybe I should focus more on being than becoming. Or perhaps I should just release myself from trying to conquer creation and instead immerse myself within its ancient mountains and valleys and streams. I should join creation as it sleeps and thrives, as it groans and heals and restores. Despite my ability to question and wonder, I'm still a creature of my Creator. And it is God who is ultimately responsible for making me what I should be.

So, this New Year's Day I shall embrace my *Come Here* status. We have come here to Highland County Virginia, and who knows what this new year holds in store?

My self-confidence at this moment isn't terribly high. But I can rest in the fact that these high Virginia mountains can't compare to the heights of wisdom in the plans of my Creator.

If I've simply come here to be...then what's to come is in his hands, not mine.

# THE PARACLETE'S APPRENTICE

I know this will sound odd and abundantly narcissistic, but I was given a new burst of life the other day by my own preaching.

I was sitting there rotting within one of my pandemic-induced funks when I decided to listen to a sermon from the church I recently pastored in Honduras. I listened to one. Then another. And the thought actually popped into my head, "This is really good!"

Of course, the absurdity of that thought wasn't lost on me. But it still felt true—not as some desperate self-affirmation, but like an out-of-body experience where I heard someone speak other than me.

How could this be?

For one, I was mainly encouraged hearing God's words, not mine. God's Word breathes life just as God breathes life.

And I was reminded of this: God is able to use me in a way that transcends my faults—including the assumption that all my past efforts for him have been in vain.

## SLOW-COOKED PITY

I returned from Honduras with a sense of failure, that I didn't measure up to lead as a pastor should. I didn't feel I failed in every way. Fruits from my efforts were clear and abundant. But I feared my spiritual gifts had little merit in light of a wanting character—a lack of leadership skill and dedication to stick it out when the going got tough.

And then upon returning to the States there ensued the crock pot, slow-cooked navel-gazing generated by the Coronavirus lockdown, and my internal thought-life became even more searing:

*What was I thinking that I could lead anyone toward anything holy? Was I even a Christian at all? Maybe all these years I've been one of those con men Jesus mentions who's put on a good face and acted the part, but never really knew him.*

Then the other day I listened to my sermons and uncovered some plot-twisting hard evidence: success in doing anything for God has far more to do with surrendering to his vision and ways than striving in our own efforts.

And every time we acknowledge this truth, we witness an unfathomable miracle.

## DON'T MOVE UNTIL YOU SEE IT

In the film *Searching for Bobby Fischer*, a young chess prodigy learns a lesson about how to win the game. He's told he must first see the whole chessboard, projecting himself out beyond one move to every necessary move. In essence, he must use a godlike vision to guide his play. And he shouldn't move until he sees it.[1]

In Honduras when I faced the daunting task all pastors face—coming up with a weekly sermon that would find the hearers changed and enjoy heaven's approval—I often used this strategy, albeit with a few modifications.

Even the most seasoned pastors face the end of themselves when trying to communicate anything worthwhile for God. What business do we have speaking for the *Burning Bush* to guide others in an upward calling? I felt this every week I sat down to plan my sermons. But then I'd remember: I must surrender my striving.

So, I'd pray. And I'd acknowledge that God cared far more about blessing the church he'd called me to serve than coddling my insecurities. Then, every single time, a divine coin was dropped into the pit of my stomach. *I saw it.* I didn't always know what *it* was until the sermon was finished. But I could begin in earnest because God's Spirit was an ever-present help in my time of trouble.

## THE PARACLETE'S APPRENTICE

Unless we're a master chess player or God himself, none of us can see the whole board or guide our steps, knowing the result of every move we make. We have no godlike vision to foresee every outcome and would probably still self-destruct in winning the game if we did. At best we should adopt the humility of the novice apprentice with our mouths closed and ears open to hear the voice of the Master, God's Holy Spirit (known as the "Paraclete" in the Bible's original Greek).

Listening to my sermons reminded me that God is both the end and the beginning. The power I heard in those words came from the same source that gave the sermons their birth. It wasn't me. It wasn't my power. But I was a vital, collaborative assistant tasked with their delivery.

Recognizing I wasn't a fit to pastor that church long-term wasn't misguided. I do think it was appropriate to step aside and allow someone more suited than me to serve. But that didn't

mean my time there was a mistake. The Master sees the whole
board, not me.

So, my real failure wasn't in how I didn't measure up—it was
in not understanding my role. While it makes me no less valuable
or useful in God's sight, my role is to serve as more a chess piece
than a player.


## HIS GRACE NEGLECTED

> Amazing grace, how sweet the sound, that
> saved a wretch like me. I once was lost,
> but now am found. Was blind, but now I
> see.[2]


While they too often get the most press in Christian circles,
pastors aren't the only ones called to do great things for God:

The mother of a young child, brought to her knees by the
heart-wrenching duty of seeing her dear one safe and well-loved;
the man wracked by shame or addiction, facing the impossible
task of finding healing and lasting freedom; the high school or
college student desperate to make their future count; the
husband or wife feeling helpless to love their spouse in the way
they deserve.

The list runs over into every vocation, every person, every
relationship, into every meaningful task. We're all helpless to see
the whole board, to win the game. We waste so much time evalu-
ating our performance when, as always, it's surrendering our
feeble power to overcome that opens the door to God's amazing
grace.

Why do we so often neglect his grace? He is there. Every
week. Every day. Every moment. Waiting for us to surrender our
striving. Waiting to drop his divine coin into the pit of our stom-

ach, to jump-start our souls into moving toward the next impossible task—not in spite of our weakness, but because of it.

Don't move until you see it.

# PART VIII
# A DESTINATION THAT HAS NO END

At the end of your journey, you'll finally reach your destination. But will your destination be the end?

For many, death is the end. And like the path unto life, their earthly journey is much the same as their destination. They live only to survive. They assume the worst in others and themselves. They seal a casket of bitterness around their shame and sorrow. They've always felt fated to curl up and die, so when death finally comes, it's just a prophecy fulfilled.

But if your destination is eternal life, what then? Is death just to be ignored? Is it merely a small speed bump on your way to the gates of glory? Or is there a role death is meant to play in your journey?

Usually, our most common encounters with death are when we lose someone else.

Enduring another's suffering and death can feel like surgery without anesthetic. The loss invades without mercy. It impales our soul. It feels as if we've died, too. So, while many will feel comfort when someone has passed into God's eternal presence, most won't truly rejoice. Death is the enemy. It dishonors the magnitude of our loss when we assume otherwise.

However, while enduring that loss, it is still possible to learn from death. To see it for what it is. To recognize its power to shape and transform us when we allow mourning to do its work.

While it never feels like it while you're in it (nor should it), mourning can ultimately be redemptive. The body must first feel pain in order to heal. The soul must be emptied in order to be filled. This, too, is part of the journey.

Experiencing death helps you treasure those you love and the life you've been given. And once it's had time to germinate within your heart, mourning can bloom into a genuine hope for what's ahead, a hope rooted at the deepest level because it comes from the place of hopelessness.

We don't want to live as if death will be the end. But so often we expend all our mental efforts to avoid this irrefutable fact: *death must precede resurrection.* Jesus had to die before the journey unto life would be open for you and me. Likewise, we must experience death—the death of others, but also the death of our sin, the death of our perspective on life itself—to better appreciate the life we've been given.

These final reflections honor the journey of loss, suffering, and death, the need to mourn, and the revolutionary mystery that only by experiencing death can we fully embrace eternal life—this destination that has no end.

# HUMILITY AND GRATITUDE

A beautiful woman died the other day. And for my own life, I have no reason at all to complain.

Jacqui was to turn twenty-eight in a month or so. She was a gorgeous, petite young woman with striking eyes and auburn hair. She was filled with love and with an amazing energy for life. She was married just under two years to a wonderful man. But she died. Of cancer.

I went to her funeral with that sick feeling in my stomach. Why this tragedy? Why would God allow such a wonderful young woman to be taken so soon? The injustice seemed too excessive to fathom. I imagined we'd all cry out to God: "How could you do this?" We'd shake our fists at heaven, condemning God for his rank stupidity and carelessness.

But what awaited me at the funeral was something altogether different: no bitter jury of vindictive God-haters, but a group of family and friends who, while deep in mourning, had come to certify a miracle. Through personal stories and the pastor's eulogy, I was reminded that Jacqui's life, although way too short, was one of victory. And even the tragedy of death couldn't diminish that.

According to her own public testimony, Jacqui had been delivered from a past of hopelessness where—though living and breathing—she was already dead to anything that mattered.

She had a baby daughter while still in her teens. But her life then was devoted to the numb pleasure of drugs, recklessness, and superficial relationships. The authorities eventually had to intervene, removing her daughter, and so the one good thing she'd produced in life was taken from her.

But then in her early 20s, Jacqui started attending church and the miracle slowly began to happen. Over time, she realized there was more to life than her self-destructive desires. That no matter who she'd been, God wanted to breathe into her a new life and a fresh start. She became free of the drugs, met and married a man who didn't run when things got tough, and finally achieved a goal she once thought impossible—she was given her daughter back again.

Sitting at her funeral, I was reminded that Jacqui embodied two characteristics I've found crucial to living a life of meaning: *humility and gratitude.*

Jacqui was humble. After committing herself to God and recognizing her transformation, she knew any value she had came solely from him. She once offered to help out around the church but asked if she could serve unseen. Her change was long and tedious, but she stuck to it. At one point she was feeling the desire to do drugs again, so she entered rehab of her own accord. Her humility strengthened her resolve to rise above who she had once been.

And Jacqui was grateful. She knew what a gift this second chance was—no matter what lay ahead, she'd never take it for granted. So, when she was diagnosed with non-Hodgkin Lymphoma and told her body was failing her, her gratitude only increased in measure.

In the latter stages of her illness when all physical hope was lost, she shared a passage of Scripture with a friend that had encouraged her deeply.

> *We have this treasure in jars of clay to show that this all-surpassing power is from God and not from us. We are hard pressed on every side, but not crushed; perplexed, but not in despair; persecuted, but not abandoned; struck down, but not destroyed...*
>
> *All this is for your benefit, so that the grace that is reaching more and more people may cause thanksgiving to overflow to the glory of God.*
>
> *Therefore, we do not lose heart. Though outwardly we are wasting away, yet inwardly we are being renewed day by day. For our light and momentary troubles are achieving for us an eternal glory that far outweighs them all. So, we fix our eyes not on what is seen, but on what is unseen. For what is seen is temporary, but what is unseen is eternal. (2 Corinthians 4:7-9,15-18 NIV)*

Jacqui knew that none of us are guaranteed our next breath— so we should be grateful for the life we've been given. And because of her commitment to God, she knew the life she'd been given would begin anew after this light and momentary trouble was through. And that her miraculous transformation of character, her new husband, the return of her daughter, were just a small taste of what that new life would be. Jacqui was humble. She was grateful.

THE LESSONS GLEANED from Jacqui's life and death remind me of the smallness of my perspective. I so often gripe about the slightest offense or silliest disappointment. But for my own life, I just have no reason to complain.

When I'm feeling down about my place in life, not getting my just due, or even about how God could allow someone like Jacqui to suffer and die, there are specific traits missing from my psyche. I'm not humble. And I'm not grateful. When I get honest with myself, I have far more reasons to be humble and grateful than I have reasons to complain. My perspective must be about who I am before God in light of eternity more than in this short visit to planet Earth.

If you find yourself dissatisfied with where you are, or worse, if you're in the pit of depression, despair, or bitterness—this might seem like a tall order. But it is possible. It can begin with a single shift of focus, and you can grow from there.

So, I'll start with Jacqui. I am humbled by her miraculous life and am most grateful to have known her.

And now, not surprisingly, my life is a great deal brighter having entertained that thought.

# A FRAIL AND WONDROUS THING

Today, I'm in mourning.

I feel a dense pressure in my chest not unlike a heart attack. I've cried more in the last few days than I have in years. My emotions go from disorientation to shock, from guilt to a sense of peace.

I'm in mourning because sometime last night, I lost one of the best friends I've ever had.

This friend was my cat, Figaro.

Now, before you roll your eyes and go in search of something less melodramatic, let me tell you a few things.

I too was floored at how deep my reaction was to Figaro's diagnosis and passing. Why was I so impacted by the thought of his death? Then, I remembered: as both animal lover and introvert, I have few close friends. Also, my wife and I have no children, so our connection to Figaro was more parent-child. And among all the pets we've owned, Fig has always been one of the most special. So, his passing struck me at least as hard as any human death I've experienced.

Learning he'd die soon, I even emulated his physical symptoms. My throat swelled. I was lethargic and rigid. I developed a fever and other severe ailments. At some point just before dawn this morning, my symptoms subsided. So I knew he was probably gone.

Many of you have faced the death of a human loved one and I would never claim you should place this on the same level. The point is, you shouldn't, but for whatever reason, I have. So whether pet or a human, perhaps you'll find some parallels here. It's caused me to consider the implications of the life and death of anyone we've loved.

HOW IT IS possible to reconcile the immense joy I've felt with Fig in my life and the vile pain of watching him fade away? It feels so offensive that such extremes should exist in the same relationship. What is the point of experiencing such joy with anyone if they are just going to be ripped away by sickness and death? It makes no sense.

One thought, of course, is that it's not supposed to. Call it one of life's great mysteries. Or that God never intended death and suffering in the first place—they were the result of man separating himself from his Creator. So maybe it's best for me just to pray for a pet heaven and rejoice that God has it all in control.

While I believe such thoughts can be helpful, I don't believe mourning is meant to be that simple. One of my favorite movies is *Shadowlands*, the story of how C.S. Lewis meets and marries a woman only to lose her to cancer. At one point before her death, his wife wants to speak to him about her passing, but Lewis objects. She tells him, "We can't have the happiness of yesterday without the pain of today. That's the deal."[1] After he's lost his wife, Lewis repeats the sentiment in this way: "Why love if losing hurts so much? I have no answers anymore: only the life I have lived...The pain now is part of the happiness then. That's the deal."[2]

I don't believe God caused the pain and suffering that comes with this fallen world, but he has decided to enter into both our joy and our pain—and that somehow sanctifies both. There will be a day without sorrow, but that day isn't today. So while I'll never call sickness and death "good," they are part of the hand we're dealt when we choose to love and be loved. In this sense, we should embrace mourning with as much devotion as we embrace joy.

As humans, we're a mixed bag of life and death, love and hate, joy and pain. The joy we feel would seem a little less precious if there were no cost, if there were no limitation or end to it. Life then becomes a frail and wondrous thing to be valued above all other things. We must experience pain and death, I think, to catch a better glimpse of that.

I WOKE up at one point early this morning to see the bathroom light on, the door closed. My wife, who loved Figaro as much as I did, was in there penning a poem for him.

Later, we wrapped him in a towel, placed him in his box, and set near him a small teddy bear, some play string, a jingly ball, and some cat treats. Before also placing the poem in the box, my wife read it to him aloud:

Here lies Figarodeo,
    Coolest cat I've ever known.
    You loved singing along
    To "Strangers in the Night."
    Elevator rides, staying in the garden all night.

The finger game,
>Making the bed,
>Following us on walks,
>Sleeping on the edge.

The "spot of the week" was your
>Favorite place to nap,
>Except when cuddle emergencies would strike,
>Then it was sprint...tackle—straight to a lap.

The only cat I know who would
>Always come around
>To greet you for his nap pickup
>To get carried upside down.

A force to be reckoned with—
>Ten pounds of fluff.
>We learned to respect
>When you had to be tough.

"Don't touch me" kitty,
>We dared not embrace.
>Big stray dogs
>Out of the yard, you would chase.

You were not just a cat.
>You were our very best friend.
>If animals go to heaven,
>Surely we'll see you again.

No more "Figgage."
>No more fluffy kitty,
>With the beautiful face

And gray-tipped hair
That made you so pretty.

I didn't think we'd have to say goodbye to you so soon.
An enormous chunk of our hearts is going with you.

The pain and the happiness—that's the deal.

# THE GREATEST OF THESE

*Love never fails. But...whether there is knowledge, it will vanish away...*
*For now we see in a mirror dimly, but then face to face. Now I know in part,*
*but then I shall know just as I also am known. Now abide faith, hope, love,*
*these three; but the greatest of these is love. (1 Corinthians 13:8,12 NKJV)*

The greatest of these is love. When knowledge vanishes and faith and hope are tested, love can fill the depths of our need, coloring our perspective with the hue of what's important, what is lasting. And love can give us a reason to live when everything else falls away.

Alzheimer's disease is a vile falling away. It strips a person of their *personhood*—their connection to the world and other human beings. But equally tragic, it assaults not just the victims, but those who love them as well. Of course, all serious illnesses have this effect. But unlike diseases that take a loved one far too soon, Alzheimer's often lingers, slowly eroding a person's essence while keeping their body intact for years.

So the story of Alzheimer's must include the families, the caregivers, as well as the victim. And understandably, the conclusions drawn will differ depending on the effects of the disease and the personalities, backgrounds, and beliefs of those involved. But the one constant, at least in the following testimonies, is the greatest of these—love.

Here are three stories:[1]


## BETTY

"My whole life, I've called her Mama. Now I just call her Mom," my wife, Zolla, realized recently. Her mother, Betty Wadsworth, 76, was only a few years ago diagnosed with Alzheimer's.

Zolla's sister, Joyce, is one of their mother's primary care-givers, along with another sister, Noretta. Other family members pitch in when they can—eight children in all.

Joyce describes the day Betty was diagnosed:

> [The doctor] asked her if she had any children. She hummed around a bit then decided, yes, she had some children. He asked her to name her children, and she looked over at me and said, "There's one...Ask her."

Such playful remarks have been a trademark of Betty's life long before they were mixed with such bittersweet irony. Alzheimer's can alter the personality as well as the intellect. But while the disease has diminished Betty's mental confidence to articulate what's important to her, her endearing, gentle person-ality remains untouched.

Says Joyce:

> We've learned things from Mom. We have learned that, even when she doesn't have her mind, she is still sweet and kind and loving. I don't know that I'd pass that test.

And yet her children mourn the loss of a woman who is still very much alive. Not having the closest emotional bond with their mother, Joyce describes how they bonded instead through mutual experiences, and how they are sorely missed:

> She would always do fun things with us: projects, quilting, cooking. I grieve her loss of ability to cook and be artistic, her love of gardening, her creativity as an expression of herself.

One ability that does remain, however, is seen in Betty's devotional adoration for God. Where her vocabulary has diminished in most other areas, Betty can still sing church hymns from beginning to end with only occasional difficulty. Joyce says:

> She likes being in church. Although, it makes her nervous when people come up and say hello because she doesn't know who they are. Then she gets close and sticks real close to me. But when she sees her sister, Nora Belle, she'll literally run across the room and give her a kiss.

As with the hymns of God are Betty's childhood memories. Forgetting the names of most everyone else around her, Betty can still name her brothers and sisters. Like many stricken with Alzheimer's, Betty's short-term memory has been replaced by an awareness of long ago, when she was bursting with the potential of youth, and life was more simple and secure.

Her sister, Nora Belle, describes a time recently when she tried to read the Bible with Betty and felt a painful difference:

> It was terribly difficult. In childhood, I would sit next to her in Sunday School because I was afraid I wouldn't know a word when they called on me to read. I would sit next to her because she would always tell me the word. And I thought when we were sitting there reading: *This is strange. Now, I'm telling her.* And, that never, never occurred. She was always the one helping me.

Alzheimer's is a genetic disease, so Nora Belle is relieved not to have seen any sign of it in her own life. But Betty's illness has been next in a series of cases seen in their family, including their own mother, aunt, and grandfather. So, for Betty's children, there is the added burden of not only seeing their mom fade away, but fearing for their own futures as well.

Joyce muses:

> We are so fragile and don't realize it. We believe God's given us this brain and the power to think and create and choose, so we often think we're God. But we're fragile and totally dependent on God. Our ability to reason, to choose, to think is all a gift from him.

And yet with my wife's mother, despite the stark symbolism of her illness, much of what's made her lovable still holds fast. Not all families are allowed this reprieve, so not all will draw the same solace. But within their sense of loss, God's redeeming hand hasn't been hard to find.

Says Joyce:

> I think having Mom in my home helped me conclude that you can't determine when it's time for somebody else to die. God can use people in all sorts of situations. He can use people to teach lessons to his children he wants to teach. Mom can still teach us things in her state of mind. Although I wouldn't want to be her, I can learn from her. She's good all the way through.

## FRANCES

Understandably, Daniel holds a slightly different view.

> I think our reflex as Christians is to look for the good in all things, but in so doing we often miss the point. The point of

suffering is not to find the beauty in it—the point of suffering is to learn to put your trust in and rely completely on God. God is more important than our pain, and he is infinitely more able to take care of us during difficult times than we can imagine.

In her ninth year since showing the first signs of Alzheimer's, Daniel's mother, Frances Dickerson, was home alone with her husband when a powerful storm blew through town. Once described as a pleasant, upbeat, even bubbly woman, Alzheimer's had beaten her kind demeanor into submission, leaving her far more anxious and fearful of the unknown, which for her had become nearly everything.

The storm came hard that night and sent her into a panic. And worse, it had been some time since she knew or trusted her husband of thirty-five years. He had become "that man" who would seemingly badger her, invade her privacy, and make her do things she didn't want to do.

Physically still a powerful woman, Frances took a kitchen knife and paced around the house, assuming various defensive postures. "She didn't recognize my dad, and she felt threatened," says Daniel. "It was then we realized we wouldn't be able to take care of her much longer. We were beginning to be at risk."

Shortly after this, they were forced to place her in the local hospital's secure wing.

Says Daniel:

We walked in the door and she knew full well where we were and why. She clung to my arm fiercely and trembled as people walked by. We made our way back to the secure area, and when the door locked behind us, she cried and clung to me and begged us with what little words she could speak. It was the most horrible thing I have ever done. I wanted to die that day.

Frances was only in her early 50s when she was released from her position as an intensive care nurse for what was then called "mental incompetence." It's rare that Alzheimer's would strike so young. Most don't start showing signs until their early to mid-60s. In those cases, the physical frailty of age coincides with the mental decay.

But Frances' physical ability remained strong for years, which made her increasingly difficult to handle. As the dementia progressed, she would often escape her family's grasp, forcing them to place an ID bracelet on her wrist so they could track her.

Daniel remembers:

> Her vocabulary was almost gone at this point. And she no longer sang in the mornings. Instead, she whistled a constant, aimless melody. She whistled constantly. Whenever you didn't hear the airy, aimless tune of her whistle, you knew something was up— she had probably just escaped.

One time Frances turned up missing for days, later found with blisters on her feet almost thirty miles from where she started. Still hoping to care for her themselves, her family placed dead-bolts on the doors to keep her from fleeing.

Then after the incident with the knife, they were forced to give up on a nine-year commitment to keep her home with the people who loved her most. In the cold halls of the nursing home, she paced and paced, often to the point of collapsing—like so many in her state, just trying to find her way home. Her physical health finally succumbing, Frances died five years later, only a few days after her 40th wedding anniversary.

The early attack of the disease and the painful change in Frances' demeanor made the fourteen-year journey especially tragic for Daniel, his father, and other siblings. To them, they'd been cheated of knowing and loving a mother who had so much life and potential, and whose time had just not yet come.

Says Daniel:

One of the more troubling parts of Alzheimer's for me is the idea that our minds are made up of chemicals. I think of my personality and my mind as something fundamental and unchanging about me. It's who I am and they can't take that away. Well in this world, they can. I can only hope my mother wasn't even here during the last five years of her incarceration on earth.

But when I reflect on my experiences taking care of my mother for nine years, I realize how much of God's strength and grace I experienced. I should have been crushed, but I came through fine. More than fine. I look back and I'm amazed at the strength and peace of mind I felt even during some of the toughest times.

Alzheimer's is a horrible, dehumanizing illness and I may never understand why my mother was struck with it. But I can say with certainty that God is a powerful refuge and he can bear all my burdens with ease. I've learned to trust in him.

## MURIEL

In 1990, Robertson McQuilkin retired from his twenty-two-year presidency at a prominent bible college to care for his wife, Muriel, who'd been stricken with Alzheimer's several years before.

Although Muriel suffered from most of the typical symptoms, she somehow still knew and fiercely depended upon the man she married. So McQuilkin gave up his career to care for his progressively fading love. Today, along with his daughter, he cares for her still, twenty-three years from the onset of her illness.

In his book, *A Promise Kept*, McQuilkin writes:

It was no great effort to do the loving thing for one who was altogether lovable. My imprisonment turned out to be a delightful liberation to love more fully than I have ever known...

Twenty summers ago, Muriel and I began our journey into the twilight. It's midnight now, at least for her. Sometimes I wonder

when dawn will break. Even the dreaded Alzheimer's disease isn't
supposed to attack so early and torment so long. Yet in her silent
world, Muriel is so content, so lovable, I sometimes pray, "Please
Lord, could you let me keep her a little longer?"[2]

THE TRAGEDIES EXPERIENCED in this fallen world are
beyond number. In the face of a tragedy such as Alzheimer's, our
faith in what is just and good is often stretched beyond the frame
of what a loving God could ever allow.

The disease is never kind. But sometimes amid the wretched-
ness there are sparks of redemptive light, offering lessons about
God's provision despite such worldly darkness. Perhaps the
greatest lesson is how so few things in this life are incorruptible,
and how God is their only source.

In the wake of our suffering, we long for those who have left
us. And we survive, knowing we have loved them well with the
love of God—the greatest of these.

# HOPE TEMPERED WITH TEARS

B ack when I trained for pastoral counseling, the spirit of this verse was often emphasized:

*Like vinegar poured on a wound, so is one who sings songs to a heavy heart.*
*(Proverbs 25:20 NIV)*

In counseling, you're taught a lot about listening and empathy. But you're especially taught not to tell a person in the pit of suffering, "The sun will come out tomorrow!" Most often that's not what they need to hear. They need you to join them in their sorrow, to feel someone is there and that they are loved.

This comes to mind when I think of the day when we commemorate the death of Jesus on the cross. We call it "Good Friday." But I doubt anyone was trying to cheer up Jesus' mother as she watched her son suffer and die. I doubt that in those moments, she thought anything about it was good.

But as Christians, we're sometimes carried away by our own hindsight. It was good, we say, because Jesus' death *resulted* in something good. We shout, "He rose from the dead just a few days later! His victory assures us that we can join God and our loved ones forever in eternity!" And yes, those are all good things. Great things.

But if we're too overzealous with such encouragement when comforting others, it can be like vinegar poured on a wound. Understandably, we struggle with this tension. Knowing that the joy of Easter awaits, knowing that eternity with God is promised through the cross of Christ, how can we comfort those who suffer with genuine sympathy and hope?

I think one clue is to understand that love is so often about tone and timing. When someone is in mourning or suffering a loss, we shouldn't rush them through it. We should join them and love them through it.

Will a new day dawn? Yes. We can offer this hope. But it should resemble the hope Jesus himself modeled while here on earth. Shortly before his own death, Jesus offered the hope of a future resurrection by raising Lazarus...but not before joining others in mourning the death of his dear friend.

Yes, Easter Sunday is coming, but it hasn't come yet. Yes, resurrection from the dead, complete victory over sin, and the end of suffering are all coming. But they haven't come yet. When they do finally come, we can rejoice in full celebration. But until then, our hope should be tempered with tears—for this world that longs to be made new.

Good Friday signifies many things. But the one closest to my heart is this: when I enter into my own seasons of mourning and suffering, I know Jesus is with me and that I am loved. Jesus is qualified to join me in my suffering because he himself suffered for the sake of love. And he's qualified to offer me hope because his comfort comes from the other side of death and suffering.

When you have nothing left and life has been robbed of meaning, you're often able to go on because you feel someone is there. Because Easter Sunday did indeed follow Good Friday over 2,000 years ago, you can know Jesus is there.

He's there with you now. And he'll be with you always. Until there's no more need to mourn.

# AFTERWORD

## THE LONGEST DAY OF THE YEAR

Today in the United States we celebrate the beginning of Summer and the "longest day of the year." Of course, a full day is still twenty-four hours. But today in our town, we'll see over fourteen hours of sunlight.

There's something vital about being "awake" as long as it's light. Jesus said we should focus on our work "while it is still day…night is coming when no one can work."[1] I have over fourteen hours of daylight today. How will I use that time?

Of course, there's still darkness in the world even during the daylight hours: violence, conflict, prejudice, apathy, loneliness, sadness. Jesus is the light of the world and calls us to be lights as well. How will I shine his light on those who suffer in darkness?

Despite the fact that from today on we'll see more darkness with the approach of Winter—despite the darkness in the world or the potential for darkness in us all—we can still live in hope, knowing that one day, darkness will be no more.

At the end of our journey, at the end of time, God's light will shine forever. There will be no more night, no curse, no tears or death or suffering. What does this tell me? That this longest day of the year can't hold a candle to a light that will last forever.

So, enjoy today's sunlight. Make the most of these precious hours. Overcome the darkness and keep moving toward the endless light of eternity.

It's time for you to go now.

Grace us with your light along the way.

# NOTES

## INTRODUCTION

1. Matthew 4:17 NASB.

## 2. THE LAST HOMELY HOUSE

1. For those unaware, the Last Homely House is mentioned in the books by J.R.R. Tolkien, *The Hobbit* and *The Lord of the Rings*. While I believe Tolkien's meaning of the word, "homely" is "welcoming" or "homelike," I take the liberty near the end of this reflection to also imply its modern meaning, "plain," "unattractive," and so on.
2. Maltbie D. Babcock, "This Is My Father's World," 1901. Music by Franklin Sheppard, 1915. Public Domain.

## 3. THIS IS MY FATHER'S WORLD

1. Maltbie D. Babcock, "This Is My Father's World," 1901. Music by Franklin Sheppard, 1915. Public Domain.
2. Ibid.

## 4. THE BLOOM OF WINTER

1. Robert Frost, "Stopping by the Woods on a Snowy Evening," *New Republic*, March 7, 1923. Public Domain.
2. Ibid. Apologies for the liberties taken with Frost's famous stanza.

## 5. FINGAL'S CAVE

1. Sir Walter Scott, *Beauties of Sir Walter Scott, Bart.*, 4th Ed. (London: Houlston & Stoneman, 1850), 132. Public Domain.
2. Edmund Burke, *A Philosophical Inquiry into the Origin of Our Ideas of the Sublime and Beautiful with an Introductory Discourse Concerning Taste, and Several Other Additions* (Gutenberg Press, 1756). Part II, Section I, 130. Public Domain.

## 6. CHARACTER AND WONDER

1. Exodus 3:11 NASB.
2. Exodus 3:12, 20 NIV.
3. Psalm 139:13-14 NASB.
4. Isaiah 9:6 NASB.

## 9. GROWING UP AGAIN

1. Charles Augustin Sainte-Beuve, quoted in *The American*, Volume XIX, No. 493, January 18, 1890, 273. Public Domain.

## 10. EIGHT QUESTIONS

1. Hebrews 4:12 NASB.

## 11. CLASS IS ALWAYS IN SESSION

1. Genesis 2:18 NASB.

## 12. RECREATIONAL VEHICLES

1. Romans 4:17.

## 15. WHAT'S YOUR WORKING RELATIONSHIP?

1. Proverbs 12:9.
2. Ephesians 6:5-8; Hebrews 6:10-12.
3. Proverbs 18:9.
4. 1 Timothy 5:13; Proverbs 26:16.
5. Luke 19:20-26.
6. Proverbs 12:27 YLT.
7. Proverbs 13:4; 21:25-26.
8. Philippians 2:12-13.
9. Acts 20:35.
10. Ephesians 4:28 NASB.

## 16. THE RESTORATION OF LOST DREAMS

1. Luke 2:29-30 NASB.

## 17. THE RING OF TRUTH

1. John Donne, "Sermon LXXX, Preached at the Funerals of Sir William Cokayne, KNT., Alderman of London, December 12, 1626," *The Works of John Donne with a Memoir of His Life, Vol. III,* Ed. Henry Alford (London: John W. Parker, West Strand, 1839), 477. Public Domain.
2. Excerpt(s) from WALKING ON WATER: REFLECTIONS ON FAITH AND ART by Madeleine L'Engle, copyright © 1980, 1998, 2001 by Crosswicks, Ltd. Used by permission of Convergent Books, an imprint of Random House, a division of Penguin Random House LLC. All rights reserved.

## 19. PAPIER-MÂCHÉ IDOLS

1. My thoughts on traveling to and from the country of Honduras is explored thoroughly in the upcoming section, "When God's Path Becomes Yours." But this reflection had a better thematic fit here.
2. Taken from John W. Michalak, *365 Devotions to Embrace What Matters Most* (Grand Rapids: Zondervan, 2015), 248. Used by permission of Thomas Nelson. www.thomasnelson.com.
3. Matthew 16:26 NKJV.

## 20. SPEAKING TRUTH TO POWER

1. A modest paraphrase of John 18:33-38 NASB.
2. *Charlotte Observer* reporter, Tim Funk, quoting Mayor, Pat McCrory. Tim Funk, "On the red carpet at Billy's bash with Palin & Co.," *Funk on Faith: A Newsy Look at Faith & Values in the Carolinas and Beyond:* funkonfaith.blogspot.com/2013/11/on-red-carpet-at-billys-bash-with-palin.html, November 15, 2013.

## VI. TRAVELING COMPANIONS ARE YOUR "WHY"

1. *Man's Search for Meaning* by Viktor E. Frankl. Copyright © 1959, 1962, 1984, 1992 by Viktor E. Frankl. Reprinted with permission from Beacon Press, Boston Massachusetts.

## 21. THE MIRACLE OF A SIMPLE GREETING

1. Genesis 2:18 NKJV.
2. This is a modern paraphrase of a quote most likely coined by the 19th century Scottish writer and minister, John Watson (pen name Ian Maclaren). Maclaren, Ian, Watson, John. *Respectable Sins* (United Kingdom: Hodder and Stoughton, 1909), 191. Public domain. See also https://quoteinvestigator. com/2010/06/29/be-kind/.
3. John 15:12-13 NASB.

## 23. FREEDOM IN RELATIONSHIP

1. This combination of paraphrase and quotation is taken from the novel, *Les Misérables* by Victor Hugo. Victor Hugo, *Les Miserables*, Translated from the French by Isabel F. Hapgood (New York: Thomas Y. Crowell & Co., 1887), 101-102. Public Domain.
2. Luke 4:18 NIV.

## VII. WHEN GOD'S PATH BECOMES YOURS

1. Hebrews 5:8 NASB.
2. Romans 8:28.

## 25. A STRANGER IN A LAND OF PROMISE

1. Hebrews 11:9 NASB.

## 26. THE THINGS WE LEAVE BEHIND

1. Luke 12:15 NIV.
2. Matthew 6:26 ESV.
3. Matthew 16:24 ESV.
4. Psalm 135:6-7 ESV.
5. Philippians 3:12 ESV.
6. Walter Rauschenbusch, *For God and the People: Prayers of the Social Awakening* (Boston: The Pilgrim Press, 1910), 47. Public Domain.

## 27. I'VE COME HERE TO BE

1. Wendell Berry, *Native Hill* (Grand Rapids: Zondervan, 2002), 185. Copyright © 2002 by Wendell Berry, from *The Art of the Commonplace: The Agrarian Essays of Wendell Berry*. Reprinted by permission of Counterpoint Press.

## 28. THE PARACLETE'S APPRENTICE

1. *Searching for Bobby Fischer*. Written and directed by Steven Zaillian. Produced by William Herbert and Scott Rudin. Paramount Pictures. 1993.
2. John Newton, "Amazing Grace," 1779. Music by William Walker, *Southern Harmony*, 1835. Public Domain.

## 30. A FRAIL AND WONDROUS THING

1. *Shadowlands*. Written by William Nicholson. Directed by Richard Attenborough. Price Entertainment. Spelling Films International. 1993. I also recommend C.S. Lewis' original book on losing his wife, *A Grief Observed*.
2. Ibid.

## 31. THE GREATEST OF THESE

1. As an outlier to most other writings in this book, this was a feature article I originally wrote for *Good News Magazine*, Tucson Arizona, in the year 2000. I own the copyright and so am re-publishing it here.
2. Some content taken from *A Promise Kept* by Robertson McQuilkin. Copyright © 1998. Used by permission of Tyndale House Publishers. All rights reserved.

## AFTERWORD

1. John 9:4 ESV.

# ACKNOWLEDGMENTS

I give thanks to God first and foremost. I breathe in and out every day because of him—everything else is gravy. Of course, if anything I write, say, or do has any meaning or impact, it's also because of him. For that and for so much more: to God be the glory.

I thank my wife, Zolla, who is God's assigned representative to me here on earth. In her words, behavior, and grace, she reminds me daily that God exists and loves me despite my imperfections. Zolla also has been my chief financial patron as an artist and minister, working a "real job" so I can do what I do for a living. If you're blessed by what I do and get to meet Zolla someday, please thank her, too.

Thanks so much to Arthur Boers for writing the foreword and helping prepare the reader for the pages that follow. I'm honored by your encouragement and for distilling so insightfully what the book is about.

I'm grateful to Diana Flegal for editing the manuscript. Like Zolla, she had to endure my eccentricities and foibles but still served the work with patience, clarity, and grace. As a respected author friend once assured me about good editors: Diana made the book better.

Thank you to Kristen Ingebretson for the beautiful cover design. I'm so pleased with your creative partnership in painting a picture for my thousand words.

Thank you to Leea at *AVL Photos* for your professional and nurturing hand in crafting my headshot and marketing photos.

Thanks to Amanda Martin for your helpful thoughts on legal

matters. You alleviated my concerns and your generosity was a reminder that God always takes care of his children.

Lastly, thanks to Don, James, and Holly for the use of your properties as a place to escape and write, and to Brian and Theresa at Panacea Coffee, where I felt at peace to edit and refine the book for publication.

# ABOUT THE AUTHOR

A seminary-trained author, speaker, and podcaster, John Michalak has spent over 25 years equipping others in the areas of spiritual life-change and authentic relationship. He recently served as Senior Pastor at Union Christian Church in Tegucigalpa, Honduras. Prior to this, John led Men of Valor's Jericho Project in Nashville, Tennessee, a prison ministry that seeks to restore incarcerated men to God and society. John currently lives with his wife and two spoiled cats near Nashville, Tennessee.

facebook.com/365devotions
twitter.com/johnmichalak
instagram.com/john.w.michalak
amazon.com/author/johnmichalak

# ALSO BY JOHN W. MICHALAK

365 Devotions to Embrace What Matters Most

## The #1 Bestselling Devotional Nationwide!
## (Early 2016)

It's said that as human beings, we spend about a third of our lives asleep. But too many of us spend the rest of our lives in a type of waking sleep, held captive by the bonds of distraction. The shiny trinkets of entertainment and materialism, the prisons of anxiety and brokenness: these hypnotize our souls into a resigned stupor where we assume we're living day-to-day, but are never truly alive.

The book *365 Devotions to Embrace What Matters Most* is less a Bible study than a conversation you might have with a friend over coffee. It invites you to devote a few moments each day to learning, or remembering, how to live life to the full.

In easy-to-understand, practical terms, it speaks to both the earnest spiritual pilgrim who needs a return to base camp, and to the person who has never given much thought to spiritual matters, but would like to explore that journey.

It's never too late to live the wide-awake, passionate life you once envisioned. Embrace what matters most, and start living a life rich with purpose, delight, and eternal meaning.

# SUBSCRIBE TO JOHN'S NEWSLETTER

Get free inspirational reflections from John as well as updates on upcoming books, his podcast, and other items of interest.

Visit embracewhatmatters.com/newsletter to subscribe.

Subscribe to spiritual meditations, guest interviews, and sermons from author and speaker, John Michalak.

1. Visit embracewhatmatters.com/podcast.
2. Click on your favorite podcast app to subscribe.

If your app isn't listed, search for "Embrace What Matters with Author and Speaker, John Michalak" in any other app of choice.

PODCAST COMPANION SERIES

In 2022, John began a podcast series related to the book you're now reading. The *Unto Life* podcast series includes spiritual meditations and guest interviews inspired by themes from the book's introduction and each section that follows. Special guests will include Christian singer-songwriters, artists, pastors, para-church ministers, authors, missionaries, and screenwriters. Visit embrace whatmatters.com/podcast to listen and subscribe.